Oxford Guide to
the Treatment of Mental
Contamination

Oxford Guides in Cognitive Behavioural Therapy

Oxford Guide to Low Intensity CBT Interventions
Bennett-Levy, Richards, Farrand, Christensen, Griffiths, Kavanagh, Klein, Lau, Proudfoot, Ritterband, Williams, and White

Oxford Guide to Imagery in Cognitive Therapy
Hackmann, Bennett-Levy, and Holmes

Oxford Guide to Metaphors in CBT
Stott, Mansell, Salkovskis, Lavender, and Cartwright-Hatton

Oxford Guide to Surviving as a CBT Therapist
Mueller, Kennerley, McManus, and Westbrook

Oxford Guide to the Treatment of Mental Contamination
Rachman, Coughtrey, Radomsky, and Shafran

Also published by Oxford University Press
Oxford Guide to Behavioural Experiments in Cognitive Therapy
Bennett-Levy, Butler, Fennell, Hackmann, Mueller, and Westbrook

Oxford Guide to the Treatment of Mental Contamination

Stanley Rachman

Anna Coughtrey

Roz Shafran

Adam Radomsky

OXFORD
UNIVERSITY PRESS

OXFORD

UNIVERSITY PRESS

Great Clarendon Street, Oxford, OX2 6DP,
United Kingdom

Oxford University Press is a department of the University of Oxford.
It furthers the University's objective of excellence in research, scholarship,
and education by publishing worldwide. Oxford is a registered trade mark of
Oxford University Press in the UK and in certain other countries

© Oxford University Press 2015

The moral rights of the authors have been asserted

First Edition published in 2015

Impression: 1

Published in the United States of America by Oxford University Press
198 Madison Avenue, New York, NY 10016, United States of America

British Library Cataloguing in Publication Data

Data available

Library of Congress Control Number: 2014945277

ISBN 978–0–19–872724–8

Printed in Great Britain by
Clays Ltd, St Ives plc

Dedication

To Emily Rachman, Tina Shafran, Doreen Radomsky, Nikolas Dixon,
and the Nightall Family.

Acknowledgments

It is with pleasure that we acknowledge the assistance and advice of many colleagues. Several of the earliest and most intriguing cases were treated in collaboration with Dr M. Whittal of the Anxiety Disorders Clinic at the University Hospital in Vancouver. Her contribution to the evolving ideas about contamination was invaluable. Other colleagues who made helpful contributions were Dr P. McLean, and Dr Clare Philips. Corinna Elliot, Eva Zysk, P. de Silva and Melanie Marks on OCD and trauma, and Paul Rozin's writings on the topic of disgust, were significant influences in the development of the concept of mental pollution.

Contents

Part 3 **Toolkit: Appendices**

Part 1

Contamination Fears

Chapter 1

Clinical Fears of Contamination

Recognition of the occurrence of mental contamination raised the need for methods to treat this disorder and the purpose of this book is to describe the nature of mental contamination and how it is treated.

The book comprises three parts. The first describes the nature of mental contamination and how to recognize it. The second provides details of general treatment procedures, followed by specific methods for managing the various manifestations of mental contamination. This part also gives a detailed account of how to assess mental contamination and how to evaluate the progress of therapy. The clinical implications of the concept of mental contamination are discussed. The final part provides a toolkit for therapists to use in their therapeutic practice. The manifestations of mental contamination and treatment techniques are illustrated by numerous case histories throughout the book. Exercises that are designed to give patients and therapists a sense of what contamination feels like are included in the text. The terms "patient," "client," and "participant" are used as appropriate.

1.1 Contamination in obsessive compulsive disorder (OCD)

Fears of contamination are important because they feature so prominently in the serious psychological disorder, OCD. They are the driving force that compels people to wash repeatedly. Cleaning compulsions are the second most common form of OCD compulsion, exceeded only by compulsive checking/doubt. In a sample of 560 people with OCD, Rasmussen and Eisen (1992) found that 50% had fears of contamination, very similar to an earlier figure of 55% compiled from a series of 82 patients seen at the Maudsley and Bethlem Hospitals in London by Rachman and Hodgson (1980). Comparable figures on the incidence of compulsive cleaning have been reported in a number of studies (Antony et al., 1998).

The cleaning compulsions are out of control, bizarre, and unadaptive. Over time, the cleaning turns robotic and stereotyped. It is not uncommon for patients to complain that they have forgotten how to wash normally, and even ask for demonstrations to remind them. Compulsive washing is so obviously abnormal that it has become almost definitional of OCD. Compulsive washing usually involves vigorous, repeated cleaning of one's hands because most of our contacts with the external world, including contacts with dirty or dangerous substances, are through our hands.

The compulsive behavior is an attempt to clean away a perceived contaminant in order to reduce or remove a significant threat. Contamination can threaten to harm one's physical health, mental health, and social life. The contaminants fall into four broad classes: disease, dirt/pollution, harmful substances, and mental contaminants.

In addition to the familiar contamination, *contact contamination*, which is caused by touching a dirty or dangerous contaminant, such as waste products, blood, or bloody items such as bandages, decaying foods, or pesticides, there is another less obvious form of contamination fear—*mental contamination*. The "mental" form arises from experiencing psychological or physical violation. The source of the contamination is *a person*, not contact with an inert inanimate substance. In contact contamination the site of the feelings of contamination is localized, usually on the hands, and is therefore accessible. In mental contamination, however, the feelings of dirtiness and pollution are diffuse, mainly internal and difficult to localize.

1.2 The nature of contamination fear

The fear of contamination is complex, powerful, probably universal, easily provoked, intense, difficult to control, extraordinarily persistent, variable in content, evident in all societies, often culturally accepted and even prescribed, and tinged with magical thinking. Usually the fear is caused by physical contact with a contaminant and spreads rapidly and widely. A fear of contamination can also be established mentally and without physical contact. Fears of contamination are more complex and subtle than they appear to be, and the concept of mental contamination opens wide the door. See Box 1.1.

Box 1.1 Four key qualities of fear of contamination

- Rapid acquisition
- Non-degradability
- Contagious
- Asymmetric

In most instances of contact contamination, the feelings of contamination are acquired rapidly, indeed instantly, after touching a tangible inanimate object or substance, or a contaminated person. The feelings spread rapidly from object to object, from person to person, from person to objects, and from objects to persons. The contagious quality of contamination is most evident among patients who fear that they are in serious danger of contracting an illness. The *fear* of being contaminated by a contagious illness is itself contagious.

People who are frightened by the wide spread of contamination live in a pervasively dangerous world. One patient described his constricted world in this way: "*As soon as I walk out of my front door it is Vietnam.*" Once the fear takes grip, their vigilance and precautionary behavior cannot keep pace with the spreading contamination, and if left untreated the fear compels them to avoid more and more places and people. There is no spontaneous braking mechanism to prevent the spread of the contamination. *Entire cities can become contaminated.*

Contamination is generally transmitted at full strength, and a small amount of contamination goes a long way (in both senses). However, there is a curious *asymmetry* in the spread of contamination. A teaspoonful of contaminated fluid is sufficient to spoil an entire barrel of clean water, but a teaspoonful of clean water will do absolutely nothing to cleanse the contents of a barrel of contaminated water.

Asymmetry is also observed in the transmission of contamination from person to person, or even from group to group. A person from a group believed to be sullied or polluted, such as an "untouchable" in

India, can contaminate someone of a higher and purer status by mere proximity (Anand, 1940). The reverse rarely occurs; a person of high status cannot "cleanse" an untouchable person by direct or indirect contact. The entry of a contaminated person into an unsullied group will contaminate the group, but the entry of a clean person into a "contaminated" group will not cleanse the group.

In large part, contamination becomes pervasive because it does not easily degrade. The qualities of non-degradability, contagion, and pervasiveness are evident in the rooms that severely affected patients keep locked for years and years in order to seal off the contamination. Intense feelings of contamination seldom degrade spontaneously, and even under treatment can be slow to diminish. Moreover, contaminants can leave traces even after the contaminated item has been removed. Tolin et al. (2004) demonstrated that contamination passes from object to object with virtually no loss of intensity. A contaminated pencil was used to touch neutral pencils, and the same level of contamination was transferred from pencil to pencil without loss of intensity. This demonstration is consistent with reports made by patients experiencing feelings of contamination. Objects that were felt to be contaminated 5, 10, even 20 years earlier retain their original level of contamination. It has now been demonstrated that feelings of *mental* contamination can be transferred in a similar manner to Tolin's pencil experiment (Coughtrey et al., 2014a), and we describe an exercise to demonstrate the phenomenon of mental contagion to help patients learn about the qualities of contamination (see Activity 2.4 on page 42).

"Spontaneous" inflations of the feelings of contamination sometimes occur, especially in cases of *mental* contamination. Changes in the patient's perceptions, memories, and cognitions about the person who is the primary source of the contamination, the violator, can inflate the contamination. Changes in the perception of secondary sources of contamination can also do it, but the largest effects occur in response to the primary source.

1.3 **Memory**

"I can never seem to find my keys, but I can surely tell you where the germs are in my home."

Most patients have an enhanced memory for contaminating cues and events and can retain a precise memory of the nature and exact whereabouts of contaminated material, even going back as far as 20 years or more. For example, a patient was able to recall the exact spot in the hospital parking lot where he had seen a discarded stained band-aid 10 years earlier. He was still avoiding the tainted area. Characteristically he was able to describe in detail the original stained band-aid, its exact location, and the position of his car.

An OCD participant in an experiment on memory said that he could recall the "*location of every chair at work (a restaurant) that has been contaminated, the type of contaminant involved, a description of the person sitting there, and what cleaners were used to remove the contaminant, over the last five years*" (Radomsky and Rachman, 1999, p.614). Others will recall the exact spot on a shelf on which a container of pesticides was briefly placed years earlier, and so forth. In these common instances, one observes a familiar combination of the non-degradable quality of the contaminant and an enhanced memory. If an item is contaminated and presents an unchanged threat, remembering its location makes good sense.

The results of this experiment by Radomsky and Rachman (1999) are consistent with clinical experience in showing that people with fears of contamination display superior recall of contaminated objects, relative to anxious participants and non-clinical controls who do not have this particular fear. The OCD participants with a fear of contamination displayed a superior memory for those items which had been touched by a "contaminated" cloth in an array of 50 items, half of which were free of contact with the contaminant. There were no differences between the three groups of participants on standard tests of memory.

The clinical observations and experimental findings which indicate superior memory among people with OCD, under specifiable conditions, are difficult to reconcile with the idea that these patients suffer from a memory deficit, probably attributable to biological abnormalities (Clark, 2004; Rachman, 1998, 2004; Radomsky and Rachman, 1999; Tallis, 1997). In OCD, memory problems are usually caused by a loss of confidence in one's memorial capacity rather than a biological deficit (Radomsky et al., 2003, 2006; Tolin et al., 2004; van den Hout and Kindt, 2003).

1.4 **Normal and abnormal feelings of contamination**

As with virtually all human fears, there is a continuum of fears of contamination, ranging from the mild and circumscribed, to moderate
fears, and ultimately to those which are abnormally intense, abnormally
extensive, and abnormally sustained by belief and conduct. Abnormally strong fears of contamination are unyielding, expansive, persistent,
commanding, contagious, and resistant to ordinary cleaning.

Not all feelings of contamination are excessive, irrational, and unadaptive. Contamination by contact with disgusting or dangerous material is a common, probably universal, experience. However, the sense of
contamination does not arise until the person passes through the earliest years of childhood. Young children attempt to touch or even eat
matter that is known by everyone else to be dangerous or disgusting.
Naturally they are ignorant of possible sources of infection, and the concept of infection. They do not avoid infectious people or materials and
display no disgust even in contact with excrement. Further, people are
tolerant of their own bodily products, and those of their infants, but are
disgusted by those of other people. Contact with the bodily products of
other people or animals usually produces feelings of disgust contamination and strong urges to clean oneself. As a rule, people believe that
anything which the body excretes must not be allowed to re-enter one's
body (Douglas, 1966).

1.5 **What causes a fear of contamination?**

As there is no a priori reason to assume that the fear of contamination
is fundamentally different from other fears, the question of causation is
approached from one of the prevailing theories of the development of
human fears, namely the three pathways of theory of fear acquisition
(Rachman, 1978, 1990). According to this theory, the three pathways
consist of conditioning, vicarious acquisition, and the transmission of
fear-inducing information. A powerful illustration of the informational
genesis of intense fear is provided by recurrent epidemics of *koro* in S.E.
Asia (Rachman, 2002). Rumours of an outbreak of *koro*, a fear of male
genital shrinkage and impending death, can cause panic. An epidemic

of *koro* was set off in Singapore by a rumour that the Vietcong had contaminated the food supply.

Each of the pathways can be illustrated by clinical examples.

In most cases it is possible to construct a cause and a path of development for the particular fear. The fear of contamination by contact with a person with HIV started for a highly sensitive person after he shared a wine glass and cigarettes with an unfamiliar person at a large, well-lubricated, rowdy, all-night party. The fear of picking up unspecified but pervasive germs led another patient to live a secluded life and wash compulsively. She had been raised by an extremely anxious mother who was constantly watchful for dangers and every day warned her to avoid touching suspect items. Clothing was washed three or four times before use, the kitchen was scrubbed down with disinfectants every day, and travel was treacherous. A reclusive patient had a dread of dirt that kept her virtually housebound. The problem arose when she had a prolonged bout of digestive problems in early adulthood and developed a fear of losing control of her bowels in public and/or exuding unpleasant smells in public. For many years, long after the digestive difficulties had been overcome, she showered compulsively and limited her excursions to a minimum. The patient carried out her shopping at unsocial hours, usually late at night. She feared a social catastrophe and attempted to avert the threat by compulsive cleaning and wide avoidance. An 18-year-old man developed a fear of touching pesticides, anti-freeze fluid, and then most other chemical products. It began when he heard that the father of a friend had committed suicide by drinking anti-freeze and was found dead in his garage. He was so shocked and frightened that he became pre-occupied with the story, even though it may well have been inaccurate, and took to washing his hands intensively. He avoided all contact with chemicals and places where chemicals were stored. Because of the fear, he avoided garages and had to arrange for other people to refuel his car.

A highly responsible woman was caring for her infant granddaughter, as promised, despite feeling ill. She had what seemed to be a bad cold (actually flu) and was sneezing and coughing but persisted in carrying out her obligations. Late that night the parents realized that the baby was struggling to breathe and rushed her to emergency. She had such a serious fever and respiratory difficulties that she was admitted to hospital for intensive treatment. The cause of the infant's illness was medically unclear, but the grandmother interpreted it as her fault, feeling that she had transmitted her flu to the child. As a result she developed a strong fear of disease contamination and took to washing repeatedly and intensively with the aid of disinfectants. She was preoccupied by the fear that she was at risk of becoming contaminated and might die. Unsurprisingly, she was terrified of transmitting diseases to her family.

Another patient developed a vicarious fear of disgust contamination after witnessing a friend slip and fall into a deep puddle of pig manure during a holiday in the countryside. The friend screamed as she fell into the puddle and after climbing out was filthy and distressed for hours. Shortly after this event the patient became highly sensitive to dirt and began washing vigorously and frequently, especially before leaving her home. Another patient developed a fear of being contaminated by dangerous substances after erroneously being told that someone had died after drinking from a bottle that contained brake fluid.

These cases illustrate the three pathways to fear—by conditioning, observational learning, and absorbing threatening negative information. The patient who dreaded touching anything even remotely connected to AIDS had developed a conditioned fear; the person who had a pervasive fear of germs was exposed to a frightened model throughout her life and was given a daily diet of frightening information; the reclusive patient's fear was a combination of conditioning and negative information that she had picked up when attempting to cope with her medical problem; the person who avoided contact with chemical products developed a fear of chemical contamination as a result of disturbing negative information.

A full account of the status of the fear-acquisition theory is provided elsewhere (Rachman, 1990, 2004, 2013) and for present purposes three points merit attention. First, a fear of being contaminated by contact with a suspect item can be generated by the transmission of threatening information. Second, a fear of contamination assuredly can be generated by observing the frightened reactions of other people to actual or threatened contact with a notorious contaminant. Third, conditioning processes can establish disgust-reactions in a manner comparable to conditioned fear reactions. It is probable that fear and disgust can be simultaneously conditioned. Recognition of the occurrence of mental contamination, a fear of being harmed by contamination, which results from a psychological or physical violation, requires the addition of a fourth pathway to the acquisition of fear—namely via physical or psychological violation. Psychological/emotional violation, in which "no skin is broken," can be as damaging as physical abuse.

It has been proposed that certain fears, such as a fear of deep water, might arise without any relevant learning experiences; they have always been present. Poulton and Menzies (2002) set out a plausible case for some of these "non-associative" fears (see Craske, 2003, for a critical view).

1.6 **The consequences of a fear of contamination**

The strength and depth of contamination fears is evident from the wide-ranging consequences which follow the emergence of such fears. The consequences are cognitive, emotional, perceptual, social, and behavioral. Affected people construe the world and themselves in a changed fashion. They become highly sensitive to possible threats of contamination, and the result is hypervigilance. The parameters of danger are expanded and the areas of safety are newly constrained. Memories of contamination-relevant situations or events are enhanced. They believe that they are especially vulnerable to contamination and its anticipated effects.

In cases of contact contamination, elevated attention is concentrated predominantly on external cues, such as dirty bandages, but can include the scanning for internal cues of contamination, dirt/infection. "Am I now entirely, certainly, safely clean? Does my body feel absolutely clean?" As with other fears, it gives rise to consistent overpredictions of both the likelihood of experiencing fear and the intensity of the expected fear (Rachman, 2004). "If I visit my relative in hospital I am certain to feel extremely frightened of becoming contaminated."

A fear of contamination can lead to intense social anxiety and avoidance. Patients who fear their own bodily pollution can become acutely sensitive to the effects of their pollution on other people. Given their beliefs about the pollution, it is not unreasonable for them to dread how people will react to it, and they anticipate rejection. People who are especially sensitive to negative evaluations are likely to be particularly vulnerable. Another social threat, seen most strongly among people with an inflated sense of responsibility, is the dread of passing the contamination on to other people and therefore endangering them. In these instances the usual fear and avoidance is accompanied by guilt.

In cases of mental contamination the elevated vigilance focuses on the violator, people, and places that are closely associated with him/her and can also include internal scanning of the body to try to detect signs of persisting contamination. In cases of morphing, anyone who possesses and/or displays the undesirable characteristics that the patient dreads he might acquire, or worse that might intrude into his mind or personality, is strictly avoided. The consequences of feelings of self-contamination include guilt, self-criticism and doubt, and concealment.

1.7 Methods of coping

In cases of contact contamination the fear of being contaminated generates powerful urges that can dominate other considerations. Affected people try to avoid touching anything until they have cleaned themselves. Attempts to clean oneself, and one's possessions such as vehicles and clothing, are compulsive in that they are: driven by powerful urges, commanding, very hard to resist, repetitive, and recognized by the affected person to be extreme and at least partly irrational. The most common form of compulsive cleaning is repeated handwashing, which typically is meticulous, ritualistic, unchanging, difficult to control, and so thorough that it is repeated again and again, even though it abraids the skin. There are instances in which patients continue washing despite the reddening of the water caused by their bleeding hands.

Paradoxically, the compulsive washing causes dryness of the skin because it removes natural oils and the person's skin becomes blotchy, dry, and cracked, especially between the fingers. If the core fear is that one's health might be endangered by contact with contamination material, it is common to overuse disinfectants, supposedly anti-bacterial soaps, and very hot water.

In addition to the need to remove a present threat of contamination by cleaning it away, compulsive cleaning is carried out in order to prevent the spread of the contamination. *"If I do not clean my hands thoroughly I will spread the contamination throughout the house."* Other attempts to prevent contamination include the use of protective clothing (e.g., gloves, keeping outdoor clothing and indoor clothing separated, using tissues to handle faucets, door handles, and toilet handles) and taking care to remove sources of potential contamination, such as pesticides and anti-freeze fluid.

In the process of avoiding contamination the person steadily sculpts a secure environment, establishing some sanctuaries. As the number of safe places shrinks, one's own room tends to evolve into a personal sanctuary and great care is taken to ensure that it remains uncontaminated. The home as a whole is safe but less safe than one's room because other members of the family do not share the patient's super-sensitivity to contamination, and care less about taking precautions. At the other extreme of the continuum there are highly contaminated places, such as public lavatories and clinics for the care of people with sexually transmitted diseases.

The fear of contamination generates elaborate and vigorous attempts to avoid coming into contact with perceived contaminants. An otherwise well-adjusted woman developed an intense fear of being contaminated by any bodily waste matter, animal or human. She became hypervigilant and avoidant, but on one fateful day she woke up to find that a dog had defecated on the lawn directly outside her front door. She was shocked and felt thoroughly contaminated. Repeated showers relieved her not, and within days she dreaded leaving or returning to her house (now using only the back door). The fear became so intense that she sold her house and moved into a rented home in another suburb. As this failed to help her, she decided to move to another city, and forever avoided going anywhere near the city in which the trigger event had occurred; she regarded the entire city as contaminated. Her extreme avoidance illustrates the rapid and uncontrolled spread of dreaded contamination.

Among people who have an inflated sense of responsibility, a major factor in many instances of OCD (Salkovskis, 1985), their fear of contamination, is manifested in the usual compulsive cleaning, but they also exert special efforts to prevent the spread of contamination. They are strongly motivated to protect other people from the dangers of contamination and strive to maintain a contamination-free environment. They try to ensure that the kitchen and all eating implements are totally free of germs, dirt, and tainted food. One father insisted on sterilizing his baby daughter's feeding bottles at least ten times before re-use. Affected people try to ensure that their hands are completely free of contamination before touching other people or their possessions. If they feel that they have not been sufficiently careful, anxiety and guilt arise. They try to recruit the cooperation of relatives and friends in preventing and avoiding contamination, but seldom succeed in persuading adults to comply with their excessive and irrational requests.

People who feel that their cleaning and avoidance behavior have not ruled out the threat from contamination resort to neutralizing behavior and/or a compulsive search for reassurance. Coping with a fear of *mental* contamination, however, presents some problems. The content and intensity of the fear can be changeable and puzzling because of the obscurity of the contaminants. What is provoking the feelings and how does the contamination arise even without touching dirt or germs? Repeated cleaning is the most common attempt at coping, and can achieve temporary relief but is ultimately futile because the contamination is not confined to one's hands; it is not localized. Therefore the patients resort to other means of neutralizing their feelings and fears. These tend to take the form of internal neutralizing, and include counting, praying, or repetitious phrases. In some cases of mental contamination, attempts to cleanse one's mind are added to the familiar methods of escape and avoidance and some patients drink water to flush out the perceived dirt.

Feelings of mental pollution/contamination often have a moral element, and theologians who recognized "mental pollution" hundreds of years ago are the experts in this domain. When pollution occurs after an objectionable impure thought or act, or contact with an impure place/material/person, the religious advice or requirement is that the person carries out a ritualistic cleansing of one's body, and secondarily of one's possessions and surroundings. The religious tactics to overcome or at least subdue the feelings of mental pollution include prayers, pardons, offerings, resolutions, disclosures, compensations, acts of charity, acts of service, confessions, inhibition, exorcism, repentance, and renunciations. This list is not immediately familiar to clinicians.

1.8 **Disgust, fear, and contamination**

Fear and disgust are intense and unpleasant emotions. With a few exceptional instances of pleasurable fear, these emotions are aversive and people exert considerable efforts to escape from or avoid them. Laboratory research shows that disgust and a fear of contamination are moderately associated (Deacon and Olatunji, 2007; Woody and Teachman, 2000), and an overlap between fear and disgust is observed in some instances of OCD. In an experiment with non-clinical participants, Edwards and Salkovskis (2005) found that an induced increase in fear of spiders was followed by an increase in disgust. However, an increase in disgust left the level of fear unaffected. They concluded that "disgust reactions are magnified by fear, but fear is not magnified by disgust." There are exceptions in cases of mental contamination in which disgust inflates a fear of the violator.

In both fear and disgust the emotion can be provoked by direct or indirect contact with a perceived contaminant. In both instances the observed consequences—cognitive, behavioral, and perceptual—are similar and, most prominently, both disgust and contamination-fear generate compulsive cleaning. If it is disgust contamination then soap and hot water will do, but if there is a threat of infection by contamination, disinfectants might be added. In both instances the aim is to remove the contaminant. In both instances it is believed that after contact the contamination can be spread, and in both of them attempts are made to limit or prevent this contagion. Some stimuli (e.g., dirty bandages, decaying food) can provoke both disgust and a fear of contamination. Others can provoke one or the other but not both.

There is far more disgust than contamination fear. There are innumerable stimuli or situations capable of provoking disgust that convey no threat and produce no fear. In the large majority of fears there is no element of disgust. The cues for disgust generally are olfactory and visual and include putrefaction and the stench from decaying vegetable matter and bodily waste. Smell plays little part in fear. In instances of disgust the distress is readily removed by cleaning, and once it is completed, no threat or discomfort persists. The successful removal of the contaminant can be confirmed visually and by the disappearance of the smell. Disgust contamination and fear contamination run different time courses.

In those instances of contamination which threaten one's health the problem and the fear are relieved but not removed even after full cleaning. The possibility that one might have been infected by contact with a harmful contaminant cannot be adequately resolved by cleaning, as in fears of AIDS. Unlike disgust contamination, the triggers for the fear of being infected by a contaminant are not always identifiable. The suspect viruses or germs are invisible and difficult to remove with certainty. The threat of becoming ill or suffering from a disease is not imminent but is persistent and generates fear and doubt. Disease contamination is accompanied and followed by considerable doubting in a manner that seldom occurs in disgust reactions.

The facial expressions associated with disgust and fear differ, as do the physiological reactions that accompany the two emotions. The physical reactions to stimuli that evoke disgust include an array of gastric sensations such as nausea, gagging, and vomiting. Fear reactions include a pounding heart, sweating, trembling, and shortness of breath.

Fear and disgust interact in some cases of *mental* contamination. People are the primary source of the contamination, and they can be a source of disgust. Feelings of contamination after a sexual assault almost certainly have an element of disgust, mixed in with feelings of aversion and anger. It is suggested that there are elements of disgust and aversion in most, or all, instances of mental contamination caused by physical or psychological violations. In several of the case excerpts described here, these elements were explicit or implicit (e.g., in the cases of betrayal, humiliation, and assault). Understandably, in such cases it is often a feeling of angry disgust.

The relationship between disgust propensity and mental contamination was investigated in a study of 63 OCD patients by Melli et al. (2014). They found significant correlations between mental contamination, disgust propensity, and OCD symptoms, and provisionally concluded that mental contamination plays a mediating role in the relation between disgust and OCD.

1.9 Sensitivity to contamination

Most people function as if they are at a lower risk of health problems than are other people. For example, if they rate the risk of a person like themselves having a 10% risk of a significant stomach ailment over the next 10 years, they give themselves a rating of say 2%. They assume that they are less vulnerable than other people to health risks. These assumptions were described by Shelley Taylor (1989) as "adaptive fiction illusions." At the other extreme, abnormal beliefs and feelings about contamination can reach delusional levels. They often have a bizarre quality, are impervious to contradictory evidence, and tend towards permanence. Some clinical examples include: a belief that one is vulnerable to contamination from mind germs, or from the sight of physically handicapped people, or that one can develop gangrene from touching any patients in hospital. In these cases, as in others, the bizarre quality of the belief is all the more remarkable because many of the people holding such beliefs are well informed and acknowledge that their beliefs are strange and restricted to themselves. The beliefs predispose the person to the acquisition of fears of contamination.

A comprehensive account of how these beliefs are formed and consolidated is not yet available, but numbers of patients describe extraordinary parental beliefs and practices that must have sensitized them to the pervasiveness of danger. "The world is full of dangers," "Pollution and disease inhabit the world," "All public facilities are cesspits," "I must wash all of your toys in Lysol® repeatedly."

The common co-occurrence of contact and mental contamination raises the possibility of a broad sensitivity to contamination, and there is some supporting statistical evidence (Rachman, 2006). The report by Ware et al. (1994) of a significant correlation (0.34) between disgust sensitivity and the washing subscale of the Maudsley Obsessional Compulsive Inventory (MOCI) was a first step, especially as disgust did not correlate with the other subscales of the MOCI (e.g., checking). On similar lines, Sawchuk et al. (2000) found a correlation of 0.49 between disgust sensitivity and the contamination subscale of the revised MOCI, the Vancouver Obsessive Compulsive Inventory (VOCI). A recent study which validated a measure of contamination sensitivity—the Contamination Sensitivity Scale (CSS)—found that the CSS is a valid and reliable measure of a sensitivity to contamination, and that CSS scores were significantly correlated with scales assessing contact contamination, mental contamination, disgust sensitivity and anxiety sensitivity in OCD, and anxious and student samples (Radomsky et al., 2014). In addition, CSS scores were significantly higher among individuals diagnosed with OCD who reported contamination fears than those diagnosed with OCD who did not report contamination-related concerns. Interestingly, scores were also elevated (although less so) among individuals diagnosed with anxiety disorders other than OCD, indicating that a sensitivity to contamination might be a transdiagnostic quality.

The next step is the investigation of the associations between the two divisions of contamination, contact and mental, and anxiety/disgust sensitivity (AS, DS). The correlation between contact contamination and anxiety sensitivity was expected to be larger than the correlation with disgust sensitivity. In a mixed sample of clinical and non-clinical participants, the VOCI contamination scores correlated with the anxiety sensitivity index (ASI) at 0.53, $p < 0.001$, and with DS at 0.38, $p < 0.001$ (Radomsky et al., 2014). The hypothesis is that the two divisions of contamination share a common element—hypersensitivity. It is deduced that the sensitivity to contamination is related to other types of sensitivity, beginning with AS and DS, and this prediction was recently been supported by Radomsky et al. (2014) using the research scale for assessing sensitivity to contamination (CSS), that is reproduced in the Toolkit (Part 3).

The possible occurrence of elevated states of sensitivity to contamination is raised by cases in which strong feelings of contamination erupt suddenly. Not infrequently they erupt full-blown, and many neutral cues are immediately converted into contaminants. Oversensitivity might help to explain those occasions in which disproportionately strong feelings of contamination are evoked by relatively mild contaminants, by cues that ordinarily produce minimal contamination. There is no shortage of clinical examples of sudden, rapid onsets and disproportionately strong reactions.

Given the connections between OCD problems and depression, patients who have a general sensitivity to contamination might be at an elevated risk of becoming contaminated during states of low mood or frank depression.

Case illustration of fear of contamination in OCD

Ian is a man in his 40s who suffered from disabling OCD for over 20 years. His fears of contamination were so severe and widespread that he became housebound and was unable to continue working. He felt contaminated "all the time" and prior to the course of cognitive behavior therapy (CBT) was washing his hands up to 80 times per day. His hands were excoriated and twice a month his dermatologist treated them with a special cream. On retiring to bed he coated his hands with medicated cream and put on gloves to contain the cream and to prevent further contamination.

During the 20 years, Ian received a great deal of psychological and pharmacological treatment, including several courses of exposure and response prevention (ERP) and two full courses of CBT. He had also received treatment in a specialized, national OCD in-patient therapy unit on two occasions. Although he had some benefit from the treatments, the improvements soon faded and he remained in a distressed and disabled condition, frightened and housebound.

Ian was then referred to a specialist OCD out-patient clinic, and after an extensive clinical interview and the results of several psychometric tests, he was diagnosed as suffering from mental contamination. On the VOCI-Mental Contamination Scale, a questionnaire for assessing the presence of mental contamination, his score of 47 placed him in the severe category.

His OCD had developed after his wife unexpectedly sued him for divorce and he had been obliged to leave his home and was given only limited access to his very young son. Months later Ian was shocked when he learned that his wife had engaged in clandestine affairs during the marriage, and he felt deeply betrayed.

On his own initiative he arranged child-care payments, but a child support agency nevertheless started sending him increasingly intimidating demands, and his several attempts to explain the situation to a variety of government officials at the agency were dismissed "contemptuously." Ian dreaded the arrival of the brown government envelopes containing the demands, and started to wash his hands vigorously after opening the letters. The envelopes felt polluted and therefore he needed to cleanse himself. As the fear intensified he resorted to wearing thick gloves before touching the letters, washing himself and then changing into "sterile" clothing. The contagion spread to other government letters and ultimately to anything, or anyone, associated with government. Post-offices and the entire area surrounding them were particularly contagious, and he was housebound.

The first of the nine sessions of CBT, consisting of the provision of information about mental contamination and the planned treatment, was followed by in-depth cognitive analyses of the betrayal, its effects, and his current appraisal of the events and people involved. A clear connection was established between the betrayal and its humiliating and degrading consequences, and the emergence of his fear of contamination/pollution. It was established that his feelings of contamination were easily and powerfully provoked by mental events, such as images and memories, not only by actually touching the "government" cues. In session four he was asked to imagine a few scenes that were neutral and then two scenes that were related to the betrayal and humiliations. Ian was adept at forming vivid images, but the first betrayal scenes produced only a tiny change in the feelings of contamination in his hands (from 0% to 2%). However, the second image produced a remarkable increase, from 0% to 90%. He was surprised that the feelings of contamination were "All over my body, not just my hands!" and he felt polluted internally. The image was a contaminant.

The effects of this and similar images meant that he was vulnerable to the feelings of contamination anywhere at any time; the feelings were evoked by images, memories, remarks, and telephone calls, and could arise even while resting quietly at home. Moreover, contrary to his belief, the contamination was not confined to his hands. "For that reason washing your hands, however vigorously, is not effective because it is misdirected. The problem, the contamination, is not your hands. It is all over your body, even inside you." Ian then recalled that recently he had cleaned out a garbage bin without any difficulty but was certain that if it had been government property it would have provoked uncontrollable contamination.

Repeated exposures to government cues were unlikely to affect the power of the disturbing images. The intensive repeated exposures that were used in most of his previous treatments had not been successful, so a cognitive approach was adopted. A detailed analysis of his contamination-related cognitions was undertaken and a few behavioral experiments were completed. The most frequent and disturbing images were rescripted into neutral or pleasant images, and Ian was taught how to rescript for himself if necessary. This proved to be a valuable coping technique for him.

During the cognitive analyses it emerged that his reactions to contact with, or the sight of the contaminating cues, made him feel miserable and helpless. Ian's appraisal of his fear of contamination changed. It emerged that the contaminants did not evoke a threat of being physically harmed but rather that he would get emotionally upset, feeling sad and helpless. Hence the direction of therapy was modified. He learned to recognize the miserable feelings and how to cope with them.

In order to help him escape from being trapped in his home, behavioral experiments were carried out to ascertain whether the new cognitive interpretations and tactics would work outside his home. On a few excursions from his home to test the alternative explanations he discovered that when he interpreted his discomfort as a sign of danger the contamination swelled up, but when he interpreted the discomfort as a sign of feeling miserable, he could cope and reassure himself that it was transient. When he made the latter interpretation, he experienced minimal contamination. The results of the behavioral experiments helped him to overcome his fear of leaving the house and by session six of the CBT he was no longer housebound.

Proceeding along these lines he made satisfactory progress and by the end of the ninth session Ian was no longer engaging in compulsive washing and able to move about freely. He dispensed with the protective gloves that he had worn at night. The results of the post-therapy psychometric tests placed him in the non-clinical range. His score on a standard measure, the Yale–Brown Obsessive Compulsive Scale (YBOCS), declined from 34 to 8, and the Mental Contamination Scale was 29, below the clinical cut-off of 39. The improvements were stable at the 6-month follow-up, and at the 12-month follow-up his YBOCS score was 5 and his Mental Contamination Scale score was 27. Ian attributed his progress to learning about mental contamination and how the betrayal and its consequences had made him feel degraded and contaminated.

Chapter 2

Feelings and Features of Contact and Mental Contamination

2.1 Feelings of contamination

Contamination is an intense, unpleasant, and persisting feeling of having been polluted, dirtied, infected, or endangered as a result of contact, direct or indirect, with an item/place/person perceived to be impure, dirty, infectious, or dangerous. The feeling of contamination is accompanied by negative emotions, among which fear, disgust, dirtiness, moral impurity, and shame are prominent.

Typical pollutants are decaying vegetable matter, putrefying meat, urine, and excrement. Dirty/infectious contaminants include public washrooms, door-handles, blood, contact with bodily products such as blood/saliva/semen, and contact with people or places believed to be infected (e.g., hospitals, and places/people thought to be associated with sudden acute respiratory syndrome). The fear of contracting AIDS is a common problem. Potentially harmful substances such as chemicals, pesticides, and certain foods can become sources of fear contamination. The construal of contamination is based on cultural and religious beliefs and by the knowledge prevailing in the particular society. The word "dirt" is derived from *drit*, borrowed from Old Norse, meaning excrement (Ayto, 1990), and beliefs about pollution by excrement are especially disturbing and widespread, probably universal.

Strong feelings of contamination are extremely uncomfortable and can be threatening. They generate a powerful urge to clean away the contaminant, and this takes precedence over other behavior. The feelings dominate the person's thinking and actions and instigate vigorous attempts to remove the contaminant, most frequently by cleaning. "My hands feel aflame with contamination." The feeling of contamination triggers avoidance behavior and attempts at prevention by removing potential sources of contamination. The idea can be summed up in this way: "Avoid if you can, but escape if you can't." In cases of contamination it is a matter of "Avoid if you can, but wash if you can't."

Affected people attempt to prevent the spread of the contamination by "isolating" their hands, for example by using their feet or elbows to open doors. If this is not practical they might resort to protecting themselves by wearing gloves or holding tissues. A simple demonstration of this feeling and its consequences can be carried out by asking people to insert their fingers into a jar containing sticky jam. It makes them feel dirty, and so they isolate their hands, avoid touching their clothing or face and hair, and have a strong urge to wash away the offending jam.

Activity 2.1 gives an exercise that therapists can use to gain a fuller understanding of the experiences of their patients. "What does it feel like to be contaminated?"

Activity 2.1: The feeling of contact contamination

Place your fingers in a jam jar and then spread some of the jam on both hands, so that they are both sticky. Does it make you feel uncomfortable? Do you have a strong urge to clean your hands? Do you avoid touching your hair, clothing, or other possessions? Do you avoid spreading the sticky jam?

Now wash your hands thoroughly. Is it a relief? Are you now able to touch your hair, clothing, and possessions without hesitation?

Those sticky feelings and their consequences are a tame example of significant, pervasive, and persistent feelings of contamination.

If you have a friend, colleague, or family member willing to do it as well, compare the results. Different people have different reactions, but for some people, and many patients, the feelings of contamination are disturbingly strong. Consider the frustration and distress that patients suffering from intense, pervasive, and uncontrollable daily feelings of contamination have to endure.

Also, try this exercise, but wait a while before washing. For most (but not all) people, feelings of contamination and urges to wash reliably decline over time; but the amount of time it takes varies significantly from one person to the next. Behavior therapists often tell their contamination-fearful patients to simply wait until it feels better, but some patients find this unpredictability troubling.

2.2 **Types of contamination**

Patients who suffer from OCD in which contamination is a major component have a daily struggle trying to overcome intense, frightening, dominating, and pervasive feelings of this character. They go to bed each night knowing that when they wake up they will feel compelled to carry out the same compulsive washing routines all over again. They are locked in by the fear and despair of ever feeling free of the contamination.

In clinically significant fears patients believe that the infectious/polluted/dangerous substances will cause serious harm to their well-being and physical or mental health, and also present a social threat. They know that the contamination will persist until adequate cleaning has been completed, but find it difficult to achieve certainty about the sufficiency of their cleaning. They fear that unconstrained contamination might spread to other parts of their body, clothing, and possessions.

Among those many patients with OCD who are burdened by an exaggerated sense of responsibility, the fear of contaminating others is a second layer of the fear and brings additional distress and leaden guilt. It comes as no surprise that people despair over their inability to control the waves of contamination. Compulsive cleaning which overrides the person's rational appraisals is behavior that is largely out of control; it is abnormal and recognized to be abnormal. Understandably the affected people worry that they might be weird or mentally unstable because their thoughts and behavior are so irrational, uncontrollable, disturbing, and perplexing. At times they feel overwhelmed by the feelings of contamination.

Fears of contamination are classified into two groups: contact contamination and mental contamination. The familiar form, *contact contamination*, arises from physical contact with a tangible, harmful, unpleasant substance. The less obvious form, *mental contamination*, arises without physical contact. It is provoked by a person or persons, not by inanimate tangible substances. Mental contamination develops in people who have experienced a psychological or physical violation and is unique to the affected person.

There are sub-types within each group. Contact contamination is caused by physical contact with dirt such as decaying material, animal/human waste, bodily fluids, germs, or dangerous substances such as pesticides. These three types of contact contamination are distinguishable but sometimes are entangled (e.g., there are mixtures of dirt and disease; see Figure 2.1).

The second group, mental contamination, has perplexing features and is difficult to observe. The source of mental contamination is human and the feelings of pollution and mental contamination are provoked by memories, images, and thoughts. It arises from physical or psychological violation and is manifested in four ways: visual contamination, morphing, mental pollution, or self-contamination (see Figure 2.2). The affected people are usually perplexed when they begin to learn that their feelings of contamination can arise even when they have not touched a tangible contaminant. The learning process tends to be gradual, but once they grasp the nature of their mental contamination, they make sense of many puzzling experiences, past and present.

The two groups are distinguishable, but overlaps are common, especially after a physical violation such as rape, which often is followed by feelings of both contact and mental contamination (see Figure 2.3).

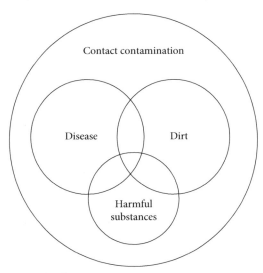

Fig. 2.1 Contact contamination.

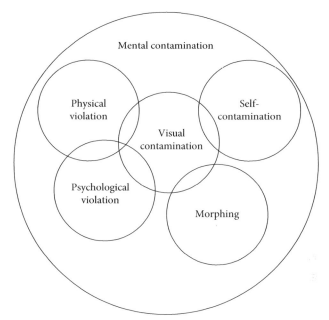

Fig. 2.2 Mental contamination.

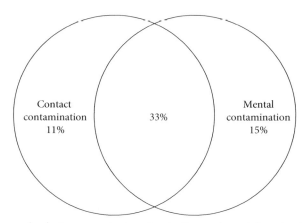

Fig. 2.3 The overlap between contact contamination and mental contamination based on a sample of 54 people with OCD. Of these, 41% did not report a fear of contamination but suffered from obsessions, compulsive checking, etc.
(Data from *Journal of Obsessive-Compulsive and Related Disorders*, 1 (4), Anna E. Coughtrey, Roz Shafran, Debbie Knibbs, and S. Rachman, Mental contamination in obsessive-compulsive disorder, pp. 244–50, 2012.)

Given this overlap, it is necessary to decide how best to treat those many patients, roughly 50%, who suffer from mental contamination or mental contamination plus contact contamination. A discussion of this important overlap, and treatment guidelines are provided in Chapter 6.

2.2.1 Contact contamination

Unpleasant feelings provoked by contact with nasty contaminants are universally experienced, and many items and places are widely recognized to be contaminated. These feelings of contamination are normal, in the sense that they are universal. Feelings of contamination that are extraordinarily intense, widespread, persisting, disturbing, and dysfunctional are a psychological problem. See Boxes 2.1 and 2.2.

2.2.2 *Mental contamination*

"This disease is beyond my practise."

Many patients suffering from OCD continue to feel dirty despite strenuous attempts to clean themselves. Taking four, five, or six hot showers in succession fails to produce the desired state of cleanliness. Why does repeated washing fail?

The concept of mental contamination was introduced as part of an attempt to explain why numerous patients with OCD express great frustration about their inability to achieve a feeling of thorough cleanliness. "*It looks clean but feels dirty*" (Rachman, 1994). Initially mental contamination was thought to be an unusual variant of contamination, but as the evidence accumulated it became evident that mental contamination is far more common than originally estimated. It is not a minor matter (Rachman, 2013b).

It is a feeling of internal dirtiness/pollution that is caused by a psychological or physical violation. The source of the pollution is human, and the affected person develops strong feelings of contamination that are evoked by direct or indirect contact with the violator. Indirect contacts include memories, images, or thoughts about the violator or the violation. For example, after a life-altering betrayal, the thoughts and

Box 2.1 Features of contact contamination

- Feelings of pollution, infection, or threat provoked by perceived contact with a source of harmful, infectious, or soiled substances (mainly concerned with dirt or disease)
- Feelings evoked instantly by contact
- Mainly focused on the skin, especially hands
- The contaminant is tangible
- The source of the danger/discomfort is known
- The discomfort of contamination dominates other behavior
- The site of the contaminant is identifiable
- Contamination spreads widely
- Does not easily degrade
- Transmissible to others
- Other people are considered to be vulnerable to the contaminant
- Associated with compulsive checking if person is prone to inflated sense of responsibility
- Anxiety is evocable by relevant memory/image of contamination
- Lacks a moral element
- Accompanied by revulsion, fear, or nausea
- Transiently responsive to cleaning
- Treatment is moderately effective

memories of the betrayal and of the betrayer can evoke intense feelings of contamination. In most instances there is a moral element involved in the violation. Commonly, the patient is unwilling or unable to say out loud the name of the violator.

Negative emotions such as disgust, fear, anger, helplessness, shame, guilt, and revulsion are associated with the contamination. These unpleasant feelings instigate attempts to clean away the contamination, but as it is mainly a sense of internal dirtiness, the site is difficult to localize and

Box 2.2 Beliefs and appraisals about contact contamination

- To avoid illness I must always handle garbage and garbage bins very carefully
- I wash my hands after handling money because it is so dirty
- I am sure to pick up a sickness whenever I travel
- I avoid public telephones because they are sources of contamination
- I worry that I might pick up contamination that will affect my health years from now
- Once contaminated, always contaminated—it doesn't go away
- If I get sick, I must make absolutely sure to avoid passing it on to other people
- Some types of contamination can cause mental instability
- I pick up infections very easily
- It is important for me to keep up to date with the latest information about germs and diseases
- I never ever feel properly clean, all over
- To be safe it is essential for me to wash my hands very thoroughly and frequently
- I am allergic to almost all chemicals
- I worry that if I get sick, I won't be able to cope
- I am responsible for keeping my home completely free of germs
- I need to be very careful to keep away from people with an obvious cold
- If I eat food that is past the due date, my stomach will get seriously upset
- To keep safe from germs it is essential to use powerful disinfectants
- When I get an illness it takes me a very long time to recover

---

Box 2.2 Beliefs and appraisals about contact contamination *(continued)*

- One can pick up sicknesses on buses because they are very dirty
- Contamination never fades away
- When I get sick, I get really sick
- For reasons of safety it is essential for me to keep everything very clean
- It is safest to avoid touching animals because they are sources of contamination
- If I thought that I had passed my sickness on to others, it would make me extremely upset
- I am much more sensitive to pollutants than most other people
- Any contact with bodily fluids (blood, saliva, sweat) can lead to infections
- To be safe I try to avoid using public toilets because they are highly contaminated
- If there is any sickness around I am sure to pick it up
- Unless I am careful to wash thoroughly I might get ill

---

hence compulsive handwashing is not effective. The source and the site of internal pollution are unclear to the affected person. See Box 2.3.

Mental contamination is specific and unique to the affected person, and is not transmissible. It can be induced or exacerbated by "mental events" such as accusations, insults, threats, humiliations, assaults, and memories and by unwanted and unacceptable thoughts and images (e.g., incestuous images, impulses to molest children). A person, object, or place that is associated with the primary (human) source of the contamination, the violator, can become a secondary source of contamination. The contaminated person avoids contact with clothing or other possessions of the violator, and tends to avoid places associated with the violator.

After a physical violation, such as rape, there is a threat to one's health and intense persisting feelings of pollution and mental distress. The feelings of pollution are intolerable and some victims of rape are convinced

Box 2.3 Pollution of the mind

The term *pollution of the mind* was used in 1666 by John Bunyan to describe his life-long affliction. An intensely religious man, he was flooded with blasphemous urges and malicious thoughts which polluted him. Lady Macbeth is a royal example of mental pollution. Although she was not present during the murder of King Duncan, she experienced intense guilt about her crucial role in his death. The intangible quality of mental contamination frustrated her attempts to remove the feelings of guilt and distress by washing her hands compulsively. It failed to give her peace or relief (Rachman, 2013a). Her nurse observed Lady Macbeth persistently rubbing her hands: "It is an accustom'd action with her, to seem thus washing her hands: I have known her continue in this a quarter of an hour," (*Macbeth*, Act 5, scene 1). Her repeated attempts to clean herself were futile. "What, will these hands ne'er be clean?" and later, "Here's the smell of blood still: all the perfumes of Arabia will not sweeten this little hand. Oh, oh, oh." Her doctor was moved: "What a sigh is there!" and he conceded that "This disease is beyond my practise."

that the traces of the violator's bodily fluids remain in or on their body for many years after the assault (Steil et al., 2011). In common with victims of other traumas they may feel irreparably damaged; for example, "I am irrevocably polluted and permanently damaged."

After a *psychological* violation the person might be left with a mixture of pollution and fear, depending on the nature of the violation. Betrayals tend to be followed by feelings of pollution, distress, self-doubt, and anger rather than fear (Rachman, 2010). Exposure to prolonged degradation is usually followed by feelings of pollution, low self-esteem, helplessness, anger, and fear. Pollution that arises after being seriously manipulated is accompanied by self-criticism and anger towards the violator, and not infrequently it prompts thoughts of retaliation or revenge.

The fear of becoming contaminated by touching or even coming into proximity of a weird, disreputable person is at bottom a fear that one's character, personality, or mental stability might be compromised by the insinuation of undesirable qualities of the "weird" person. In extreme cases the threat goes deeper and the affected person fears being transformed into someone akin to the undesirable person, a fear of morphing. In caste communities, people take great care to avoid physical contact or even remote contact with members of a lower caste, such as the "untouchables," for fear of pollution and a fall into the lower caste, a literal degradation (Human Rights Watch Report, 1999).

There is evidence that some perpetrators of unacceptable acts develop feelings of pollution (Rachman et al., 2012), but they rarely seek therapy. See Box 2.4.

Box 2.4 Beliefs and appraisals about mental contamination

- Many things look clean but feel dirty
- People should be pure in mind and in body
- Some people think I am weird because I am a clean freak
- I must always avoid people with low morals
- Before leaving home I need to make sure that I am absolutely clean
- If I think about contamination it will increase my risk of actually becoming contaminated
- Seeing disgusting pornographic material would make me feel sick and dirty
- If I touched the possessions or clothing of someone who had treated me very badly I would need to have a good wash
- People who do something immoral will be punished
- Sometimes I have a need to wash even though I know that I haven't touched anything dirty/dangerous
- If I was touched by someone who had treated me very badly it would make me feel unclean
- People who read pornography must be avoided

Box 2.4 Beliefs and appraisals about mental contamination *(continued)*

- Mixing with immoral people would definitely make me feel unclean
- I will never be forgiven for my horrible thoughts
- If I am touched by a nasty or immoral person it makes me feel very unclean
- It is quite possible to feel contaminated even without touching any contaminated material
- It is immoral for me to use bad language at any time
- Simply thinking about contamination can make me feel actually contaminated
- No matter how hard I try with my washing I never feel completely clean
- If I cannot control my nasty thoughts I will go crazy
- Simply remembering a contaminating experience can make me feel actually contaminated
- It is completely wrong for me to tell dirty jokes
- I am responsible for other people's bad behavior towards me
- When I am in a low mood I am far more sensitive to feelings of being contaminated
- I will never get rid of the feeling that I am unclean and dirty
- I definitely avoid movies that contain foul language and explicit sex scenes
- I have a hard time getting rid of the feeling that I am unclean
- People think I am weird because of my worries about dirt and diseases
- If I did something immoral it would make me feel unclean
- When I feel bad about myself, having a shower makes me feel better
- Having to listen to someone making disgusting, nasty remarks makes me feel tainted and dirty
- People will reject me if they find out about my nasty thoughts

Box 2.4 Beliefs and appraisals about mental contamination *(continued)*
◆ If a nasty, immoral person touched me I would have to wash myself thoroughly
◆ If I do not overcome my feelings of dirtiness I will become sick
◆ If I was touched by someone who behaved badly I would need to wash myself
◆ People who use disgusting language make me feel dirty and tainted

A detailed description of the properties of mental pollution and how it differs from contact contamination materials was set out in Rachman (1994) and a refined table was provided by Fairbrother et al. (2005). Prominent features of the two types of contamination are shown in Table 2.1.

Table 2.1 Prominent features of the two types of contamination

Contact contamination	Mental contamination
Feelings of discomfort/dread	Feelings of discomfort, uneasiness, dread
Provoked by contact with dirt/disease	Physical contact not necessary
Dominates other behavior	Dominates other behavior
Not applicable	Can be generated internally
Feelings evoked instantly with contact	Feelings evoked occasionally
Concentrated mainly on skin, especially the hands; localized	No typical focus; diffuse; internal
Generated by contact with external stimuli	Can be generated internally (e.g., urges, thoughts, memories, images)
Not usually generated by ill-treatment	Usually generated by perceived violation
Contaminants are dirty/harmful substances	Primary source is a person not a substance
Feeling dirty/infected	Internal dirtiness/pollution predominantly
Spreads widely	Some generalization can occur
Easily transmissable to others	Rarely transmissible to others
Other people are vulnerable to the contaminants	Unique to the affected person

Table 2.1 (continued) Prominent features of the two types of contamination

Contact contamination	Mental contamination
Source of contamination is known	Source of contamination is obscure to affected person
Site identifiable	Site inaccessible
Tangible contaminants	Intangible contaminants
Contamination re-evocable by contact with dirty/diseased source	Contamination re-evocable by contact with human source
Contamination evocable by secondary "carriers"	Contamination evocable by secondary sources, "carriers"
Common in childhood OCD	Rarely occurs in childhood
Pollution seldom re-evoked by mental events	Pollution re-evocable by relevant mental events
Anxiety evocable by relevant mental events	Anxiety evocable by relevant mental events
Lacks a moral element	Moral element common
Revulsion, disgust, nausea, fear	Anxiety, revulsion, anger, shame, guilt, disgust common
Not applicable	Level/range of contamination fluctuates in response to changes in attitude to contaminator
Generates urges to wash	Generates urges to wash
Generates urges to avoid	Generates urges to avoid
Transiently responsive to cleaning	Cleaning is ineffective
Treatment is moderately effective	Promising, specific treatment for mental contamination

Activity 2.2: The types of contamination

Attempt to integrate the information you have read about the two types of contamination with your clinical experience: try to recall some of the cases of contact contamination that you have come across in your career. Do the cases described here resonate with your clinical experience?

In retrospect, do you think that some of your patients also had feelings of mental contamination?

If yes, do you think that knowledge of mental contamination would have helped you better to understand their distress and perplexity? Would the therapy have been more effective?

Case illustrations of contamination

As you read the following cases of mental contamination, refer back to Table 2.1 to see what features of mental contamination you can identify.

Case 2.1

An academic in his 40s was fearful that he would become seriously ill unless he scrupulously avoided touching anything associated with germs. He recognized the source of his contamination, contact with tangible contaminants, and how widely the threat of contamination had spread. The patient used gloves or tissues to handle many items and washed all coins before re-using them. He washed himself for up to 3 hours a day and delayed cleaning his kitchen and bathroom because it took many exhausting hours to carry out the process safely and satisfactorily. Simply cleaning his clothing took a good deal of effort and he used his washing machine every day. The compulsive cleaning and avoidance are characteristics in cases of a fear of contamination. He derived a moderate amount of benefit from a course of exposure treatment.

Case 2.2

An adolescent developed an intense fear of getting lice in his hair. In order to protect himself and avoid contaminating other people he compulsively washed his hair several times a day. He stored his clothes in a freezer for at least 2 days before wearing them, and avoided contact with other people. This included potential therapists as he was frightened that he would contaminate them as well. The boy's unrealistic and inflated sense of responsibility added a second dimension to his fear—fear for himself and a fear of harming others. No treatment was possible and he remained fearful.

Case 2.3

A 30-year-old father became so worried about the health and safety of his three children that he developed extreme measures to protect them. His fear of accidentally contaminating them with germs or harmful substances reached such an intensity that he washed his hands up to 50 times per day, spent at least 3 hours each day cleaning the bathroom and kitchen, and maintained a constant vigilance over possible dangers. He was preoccupied with the need to protect the children at all times. As is common in cases of contact contamination, the presence of an inflated sense of responsibility generated compulsive checking to ensure that his family was safe from illness. His inflated sense of responsibility was the driving force of his OCD. After a course of exposure treatment, his fear, hypervigilance, and compulsive cleaning were reduced.

Case 2.4

A man in his mid-20s, who described himself as easily disgusted, developed an intense fear of chemical contamination after cleaning his barbecue with a powerful cleansing fluid. The fear was incited when the bathroom sink in which he had washed his hands became stained within days. The fear and consequent vigilance intensified until he was preoccupied with avoiding and removing any and all possible contaminants. He improved slightly after treatment.

Case 2.5

An architect developed feelings of disgust and fear about her bowel movements after a prolonged bout of gastric illness during which she had episodic diarrhea. She spent up to 15 minutes cleaning herself after each bowel movement and used so much toilet paper that the drains blocked repeatedly. In most instances she followed this cleaning with a lengthy hot shower. The fear of dirt contamination spread to all parts of her house, then her car, buses, and shops, and of course public toilets were unapproachable. She feared that she might inadvertently disgust or contaminate others or that they might contaminate her. She responded moderately well to a full course of exposure treatment.

These cases illustrate common features of contact contamination. After perceived contact with a tangible contaminant the person feels dirty/infected/threatened and engages in compulsive washing and avoidance of recontamination. The contamination spreads and is transmissible to others. Other people are regarded as being vulnerable to the contamination and its consequences. The contaminant is tangible and, as the site and the source are known, the contamination is accessible. It is transiently responsive to cleaning, and in many cases the fear diminishes after exposure treatment.

Case 2.6

A patient tried to reduce his feelings of dirtiness by repeatedly showering in very hot water. Despite using strong soaps and stiff brushes, he felt just as dirty at the end of each shower as he had before he began. "*No matter how many showers I take, and how hard I try, I can't get clean!*" His description is a clear illustration of the phenomenon of looking clean but feeling dirty. The feelings of dirtiness emerged after he was sharply accused of being sexually immoral. A similar description was given by a young man who had fears of contact contamination and was also tormented by self-contamination—"*I shower over and over to reduce the feeling that I am a bad person.*" Another patient who was accused of immorality by his family became overwhelmed by such intense feelings of dirtiness that he repeatedly tried to clean himself with abrasive materials which ultimately damaged his skin. His feelings of dirtiness were triggered by telephone calls, by letters from "contaminated" relatives, and related cues. The feelings of pollution were not altered by the cleaning.

Case 2.7

A 24-year-old woman complained of uncontrollable compulsive washing that blighted her every day and was threatening her job in a busy restaurant. She had strong religious and moral beliefs and was easily upset by blasphemous or salacious remarks. Her friends were careful to respect her views and chose their words accordingly. Unfortunately the voracious customers at the restaurant were less considerate and when she was exposed to rough and rude remarks it made her feel so dirty that she tried to avoid touching the used dishes and table napkins. When this was impossible she escaped to the washroom and vigorously cleaned her hands with anti-bacterial soap. On a bad day she had to repeat the compulsive washing up to 25 times, leaving her hands cracked and sore. After returning from work she felt compelled to change out of her work-clothing immediately and take a prolonged hot shower. Exposure to salacious magazines or movies produced the same reactions of discomfort and dirtiness, and outside of work she took care to avoid the proximity of unkempt people and anyone whose behavior was loud and disorderly. In this case, the primary source of the feelings of contamination was people using rough, offensive, or blasphemous language and this set off the compulsive washing. The patient made progress in treatment and, although her reactions to offensive language remained on the excessive side, she reduced the compulsive washing to tolerable levels which no longer interfered with her work. Some 4 years later the feelings of contamination and compulsive washing returned, but she overcame them after booster treatment.

Case 2.8

A young lawyer, Victoria, was under threat of losing her job because of the behavior of a colleague with whom she had to share an office for several months. The woman invaded her space, used her work materials and space without permission, and ignored her complaints. The patient described the colleague as nasty, disrespectful, overbearing, and unpleasant. "Whatever her intentions, her behavior and actions harmed me. I loathed her." During the period of maximum stress, in which she felt that she could not continue at work, but was unable to find suitable alternative employment, the patient encountered a person with a serious psychomotor disability at the entrance to the building in which she was employed. The patient felt at risk of contracting the unknown, disabling illness from the person and immediately resorted to the nearest washroom, where she cleaned herself vigorously in order to wash away any dangerous germs. However, the contamination could not be controlled and quickly spread to her office, work clothing, and then to the entire building. She was overwhelmed and began to avoid many places, colleagues who had been in contact with contamination in the building, anyone with an evident disability, and so forth. The troublesome colleague was a powerful source of contamination and contact was strictly avoided. The patient developed intense, compulsive washing, at work and at home. In order to protect her family she scrupulously removed her work clothes before entering the home after work. On weekends, holidays, and in the evenings she avoided leaving home lest she encounter disabled people or colleagues. Her fear and avoidance diminished after treatment, but she required continuing support and advice for many years.

Case 2.9

A deeply religious Catholic man sought treatment for his feelings of contamination and compulsive washing, and for his blasphemous thoughts. The trouble began 5 years earlier after he became friendly with a man who belonged to a small, fringe religious group that promoted extreme views. The patient had been drawn into the group by the strong urging of his friend, and ceased attending church, missing mass and no longer going for confession. He felt guilty about his renunciation of Catholicism and became preoccupied with his religious conflicts. After 6 months he decided that he had been misled, that the fringe group was a false religion, and that his friend was unreliable and mentally unstable. As a result, he returned to his former religious practices but remained extremely guilty about his lapse from Catholicism, and fell into repeated self-criticism. He was angry with the friend who had manipulated him and angry with himself for his own weakness. The patient tried to compensate for his lapse by resolving never to allow any irreligious thoughts to enter his mind, but his attempts to suppress the unacceptable thoughts failed and instead he was assailed by floods of intrusive thoughts and blasphemous images. He also began washing compulsively. After a course of CBT he was much improved.

Case 2.10

A woman who was sexually betrayed by her fiancé was initially angry but then became anxious and indecisive and developed feelings of contamination. Her flat, many of her clothes and other possessions, and anything associated with the former fiancé triggered the contamination, perhaps better described as pollution, and consequent washing. She also developed a compulsion to keep her possessions in fixed positions and was upset if anyone moved them even slightly. Memories, images, even conversations connected with the betrayal and its distressing consequences were sufficient to evoke the feelings of pollution. The feelings of contamination/pollution were unique to her, evoked even without physical contact, initiated by personal events, not by dangers from harmful substances, and had a strong moral element. Treatment was focused on the betrayal and its effects, supplemented later by conventional exposure exercises. She benefitted from treatment.

Case 2.11

A young immigrant woman developed intense washing and cleaning compulsions, using large quantities of powerful detergents and disinfectants, when her marriage became intolerable. She had been manipulated into an arranged marriage with an older and unsuitable man whose behavior towards her was dominating, distasteful, and insensitive. Initially she tried to make the marriage work but found his behavior increasingly repulsive, and started to avoid any physical contact with him or his belongings. It was at this time that she began to experience feelings of pollution and dirtiness, and tried to obtain relief by intensive washing. Her compulsions became overwhelming and this, combined with her despair, led to a termination of the marriage. After they separated, she avoided all contact with her former husband and his family. Any reminders of them or contacts with items or possessions associated with him or the family evoked feelings of pollution and triggered her compulsions. Eventually the entire town in which they had lived before she left him became contaminated. She felt that she had been violated by the manipulations of her husband and his family and was angry and bitter towards them. Treatment was slow and difficult, but ultimately she made significant improvements, reduced pollution, much reduced washing, and she stopped using the powerful cleaning substances. Progress in treatment was slow until the emphasis shifted from "ordinary" contact contamination to her feelings of mental pollution and their origin.

Case 2.12

In many cases of mental contamination there is a moral element. A young man sought treatment because of his overwhelming feelings of contamination, most of which were stimulated by contact with dirty substances. However, equally intense feelings of contamination were triggered by proximity to shabby and disreputable-looking, immoral people, especially if he perceived them to be addicted to drugs. Even the sight of such people induced feelings of contamination, and his immediate response to these feelings was to wash his hands intensively, repeatedly. His skin, from the finger-tips to the elbows, was abraided, red, and blotchy. His reaction to the perception of disreputable people had generalized to policemen, probation officers, and even social workers, because of their contacts with criminals, addicts, prostitutes, and so on. Anyone whom he thought might have come into contact with the disreputables was polluted. He responded well to an intensive course of CBT, and the fears of contact contamination and of mental contamination declined in parallel. His mental contamination occasionally produced secondary problems, and in one instance a policeman signalled him to pull his car over to the side of the road. The patient became extremely anxious, not about a potential booking, but because the policeman was touching his car. Worse still, when the policeman returned the patient's driving licence, he was reluctant to touch it and was forced to wrap it in a paper tissue before accepting it from the officer. There is no record of the policeman's private thoughts.

These patients dealt with ordinary dirt in a normal fashion, and none of them had elevated fears of disease. Their feelings of pollution were particular, personal, not originally provoked by physical contact with a contaminant, and unresponsive to straightforward cleaning. Other examples are described by Coughtrey et al. (2012), de Silva and M. Marks (1999), and Rachman (2006).

Activity 2.3: The feeling of mental contamination

It can be difficult to imagine the feeling of mental contamination. To illustrate it, think back to an occasion on which you were humiliated, degraded, or betrayed. Did it leave you feeling a bit polluted? When you recall the event/s does it make you feel uneasy, even a bit dirty? If so, do you have an urge to wash away the feeling?

When you visualize the person who betrayed, humiliated, or degraded you does it make you feel uneasy? Even a bit dirty? Do you have an urge to change your clothing?

Think back to an occasion on which you were standing near a person who had insulted, humiliated, degraded, or harmed you. Does that make you feel a bit polluted, even dirty? Would you like to wash your hands or have a good full cleaning session? Or change your clothing?

For some people, certain thoughts are associated with a sense of pollution, immorality, or contamination. Would you wear the clothes of a person who swears loudly, aggressively, and blasphemously in public? Or the clothes of a violent offender? Or the clothes of someone who sexually abused children? Or someone who died a violent death? If not, why not? These and similar examples can illustrate the feelings of mental contamination for your patients.

Activity 2.4: The spread of mental contamination

This is an exercise that therapists can use to gain a fuller understanding of the spread of mental contamination.

Take a pack of new pencils. Take the first pencil and rate how dirty you think it is, on a scale of 0–100. Next, try to make the pencil as contaminated as possible, without touching it. Associate it with the memories, images, and/or thoughts that made you feel dirty and contaminated in the previous exercise. How dirty is the pencil now? Next, try to transfer the contamination to the other pencils in the pack, by physically touching them to one another. Can you make the contamination spread? Does it also work if you arrange the pencils so they don't touch each other?

Chapter 3

Forms of Mental Contamination

3.1 **Physical or psychological violation**

Feelings of mental contamination can be caused by physical violation, such as a sexual assault. The initial feelings of contamination are understandable, but in many instances they persist for months or years after the assault. Victims describe a feeling of inner dirtiness ("it is under my skin") in addition to the external signs, and it is these *persisting* feelings of inner pollution which have the characteristics of mental contamination. The primary source of the pollution is a person, the dirtiness is internal and difficult to localize, inaccessible, easily re-evoked by memories or other mental events, often has a moral element, and is not properly responsive to washing.

In cases of physical violation the instigating event involves some form of contact, but re-evocations of the feelings of contamination occur without physical contact. There is an overlap between this type of mental contamination and post-traumatic stress disorder (PTSD), and a probable overlap in causes and consequences. Ehlers and Clark (2000) addressed the critical question of why affected people continue to feel threatened for lengthy periods after the traumatic event; they attribute the persistence of symptoms of PTSD to the victim's sense of a *current* threat. The threat can be an external threat, say a perceived danger to their safety, or an internal threat to themselves or their future. Ehlers and Clark postulate that the person's appraisal of the trauma plus the memories of the event combine to produce a sense of serious current threat. The threat is accompanied by intrusive images and memories, heightened arousal, and re-experiencing, and these signs reinforce the victim's feeling of a *current* threat.

Mental contamination, often associated with feelings of mental pollution, can be caused by psychological/emotional violation, without any physical contact. The list of violations is disarmingly extensive and includes degradation, humiliation, and betrayal. Why then are we not overrun by an epidemic of cases of mental pollution and contamination? Are all distressing emotional experiences potential triggers for a sense of contamination?

Most people endure distressing events at some time in their lives, and feelings of violation are not uncommon, but few people develop significant feelings of mental contamination. It is comparable to the fact that the majority of people who experience a trauma do *not* develop post-traumatic disorders (Ehlers and Clark, 2000). These are examples of human resilience.

Sexual assaults can produce a blend of physical and mental pollution (Fairbrother and Rachman, 2004). See Figure 3.1. Consistent with these findings, Badour et al. (2012) demonstrated that when participants who had experienced a sexual assault carried out an imagery procedure involving a personally relevant assault, it produced large and significant increases in disgust, feelings of dirtiness, and urges to wash. Adams et al. (2014) reported comparable results and, consistent with the literature (e.g., de Silva and Marks, 1999), found that victims of a sexual assault had high mental contamination scores, whereas victims

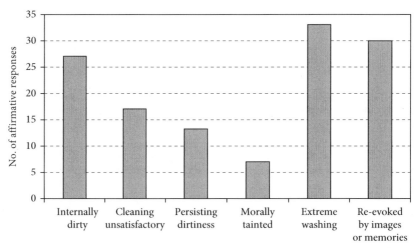

Fig. 3.1 Responses reported by 50 victims of a sexual assault. (From Fairbrother and Rachman, Behaviour Research and Therapy, 2004.)

of a physical assault did not. In addition they found that mental contamination mediated the severity of post-traumatic symptoms (see also Melli et al., 2014). In a sample of 148 participants, Ishikawa and colleagues (2013) found that perceived sexual violations predicted all of the indices of mental contamination. The most intense feelings of dirtiness occurred after rape.

Steil and colleagues (2011) conducted a pilot investigation of nine women who had experienced childhood sexual abuse and in adulthood were suffering from symptoms of traumatic stress plus feelings of being contaminated. Some of the participants were disgusted by their bodies and/or were convinced that remains of the perpetrator's bodily fluids remained in their bodies. They responded well to a combination of cognitive restructuring and imagery rescripting. In the restructuring, Steil and colleagues adroitly used physiological information to convince the participants that the dermal cells in the affected parts of their body had been completely rebuilt and hence there could not be any physical trace of the violator; skin cells rebuild every 4–6 weeks. This tactic is consistent with Rozin and Fallon's (1987) idea of "conceptual reorientation" (see Chapter 6) and is a useful addition to CBT for victims of sexual assault. Additionally, the rescripting of disturbing images is a notably effective therapeutic technique and is especially useful in cases of mental contamination.

In cases of psychological violation the victims generally recognize the injustice and immorality of the way in which they have been treated, and consequently feel anger towards the perpetrator, sometimes mixed with disgust. Violations can provoke a desire for retaliation. The perpetrator is regarded as morally repugnant. No doubt there are many instances in which the victim feels anger, repugnance, and disgust towards the perpetrator even before the trigger event/s. Being touched or manipulated or humiliated by a person one loathes may well trigger feelings of mental pollution. After being psychologically violated the victim experiences emotional distress that may include fear, anger, and disgust, and it is no surprise that they take steps to avoid seeing or hearing about the perpetrator. When these attempts fail, feelings of contamination resurge (Rachman, 2010). See Box 3.1.

Box 3.1 The features of mental contamination following ill-treatment, violation, domination, degradation, manipulation, betrayal, or humiliation

- Following an incident or period of ill-treatment the patient develops:
  - Feelings of contamination
  - Feelings of dirtiness and/or pollution
- These can arise without any physical contact with a contaminant
- The primary source of the contamination is a person/s, not a harmful or disgusting, inanimate substance
- Items, places, or people associated with the primary person/s can turn into secondary sources of contamination
- The feelings of contamination seldom degrade spontaneously
- The feelings of contamination spread
- The feelings instigate urges to clean away the perceived contamination
- The feelings promote avoidance of cues of contamination
- The feelings promote the avoidance of reminders of the incident/perpetrator and any cues/memories that are associated with the incident/period/perpetrator
- The feelings of contamination can be induced, and revived, with or without direct physical contact with items/places/people associated with the perpetrator
- These feelings of contamination are often accompanied by more familiar forms of contact contamination (from sources such as dirt, germs)
- The affected person is uniquely, specifically, vulnerable to the primary source of the contamination
- Fluctuations in the affected person's feelings/attitudes to the contaminator are followed by fluctuations in the level and range of contamination

> **Box 3.1 The features of mental contamination following ill-treatment, violation, domination, degradation, manipulation, betrayal, or humiliation** *(continued)*
>
> - The contamination is associated with a range of negative emotions and reactions that include anger, self-criticism, guilt, damaged self-esteem, and general anxiety
> - The transmissibility of the contamination has three facets:
> - Other people are not vulnerable to becoming contaminated by contact with the primary source
> - But they are vulnerable to secondary contamination, usually via the affected patient
> - People who come into contact with the primary source of the contamination can become secondary sources of contamination (carriers) for the affected patient

3.2 **Self-contamination**

Self-contamination can be caused by contacts with one's bodily products, the occurrence of unwanted, intrusive repugnant thoughts/urges, or by one's unacceptable actions. Shame and guilt are the common consequences. The intrusive thoughts that give rise to self-contamination resemble obsessions (Rachman, 2003) and the two disorders can overlap. The thoughts involved in self-contamination are obsession-like, but only a minority of obsessions produce feelings of contamination. To the extent that cases of self-contamination share some features of obsessions, the treatment focuses on the obsessions (Rachman, 2006).

Sufferers from mental contamination tend to have high personal standards, are scrupulous, and strive to maintain their moral and physical purity. Urges and thoughts of harming others, especially if the potential victims are unable to defend themselves (elderly people, children, disabled people), are particularly distressing. Repugnant intrusive thoughts and images clash with their standards and cause intense distress. They intrude, and must be blocked and suppressed, and it is essential to refrain from unacceptable actions. People who are well able to defend themselves rarely feature as victims in intrusive thoughts of harming others (see the Schwarzenegger effect; Berman et al., 2012; Rachman, 2003).

The recurrent, unwanted, repugnant thoughts and images that commonly occur are the raw material for developing obsessions are blasphemy, sexual misconduct, and harming other people. The reason why other negative socially unacceptable thoughts and actions—such as avarice, envy, gluttony, betrayal, vandalism—rarely feature as material for obsessions is a puzzle that remains to be explained. See Box 3.2.

Box 3.2 Features of self-contamination

- The person himself/herself is the source of the contamination
- Hence the opportunities for contamination and recontamination are constantly present
- Unwanted, intrusive, repugnant thoughts and urges are a major source of the feelings of contamination
- Many of the repugnant intrusions involve unwanted sexual/ religious thoughts
- Thoughts of harming other people, especially those who are unable to defend themselves, can evoke shame and feelings of pollution
- Intrusive, repugnant thoughts that cause feelings of self-contamination are concealed
- Feelings of self-contamination are influenced by mood states, especially depression
- There usually is an (im)moral element
- Repugnant habits (e.g., watching pornography) can cause feelings of contamination/pollution
- Shame, guilt, and self-distrust often accompany self-contamination
- The contamination is relevant to the patient but not to anyone else
- The appraisals of the contaminants, and their threat, are unique

3.3 **Visual contamination**

Some people are contaminated merely by the sight of a person viewed as immoral, disreputable, or bizarre. It almost seems as if the contamination magically transfers from the disreputable person into the patient. The sight of a disturbed person behaving in a bizarre manner in a public place can evoke a fear of losing one's mind. One patient gave a vivid description of how she avoided even walking in the "airstream" of a disreputable or bizarre person. Interestingly, Freud (1895, p. 88) described a patient whose phobia "was supported on the one hand by the primary and instinctive horror of insanity felt by healthy people . . . and by the fear, felt by her no less than by all neurotics, of going mad herself."

3.4 **Morphing**

Visual contamination is closely linked to morphing. The belief that the undesirable characteristics of certain people can be absorbed by physical contact or by visual contamination can generate threatening cognitions that are set off by proximity to people who are seen as marginal and include those who are perceived as mentally unstable, weird, immoral, drug addicted, or unkempt. People of elevated status rarely become the source of a fear of morphing. They are not perceived as posing any threat, and instead may prompt attempts to mimic their appearance, skills, and accomplishments. Most patients who suffer from a fear of morphing have concurrent or past fears of contact contamination or mental contamination.

The explanation for the appearance of morphing, almost like a modern manifestation of imitative sympathetic magic (Rachman, 2006), is not always clear, but in some instances it is associated with a belief in the possibility, or even probability, of the contagiousness of mental instability. If one believes that mental instability is contagious, then avoidance is understandable. An additional factor is a distaste for contact with strangers who appear to be weird or unstable, and the disgust and dirtiness that can arise after unavoidable contacts. Some patients have a history of being seriously disvalued and repeatedly told that they are failures and would come to nothing. Contact with dysfunctional people can trigger their dread of personal failure and a fear of becoming similarly dysfunctional. See Box 3.3.

Box 3.3 The main features of a fear of morphing

- The person fears that he/she might unwillingly pick up undesirable characteristics from people whom they regard as weird, mentally unstable, marginal, immoral, shabby, drug addicted, or low status
- The person fears that he/she will be adversely changed by contact with such people
- The assimilation of the unacceptable characteristics can occur as a result of touching the undesirable person or his clothing, or other possessions
- The assimilation can also occur without physical contact—notably by visual contamination
- Assimilation/exacerbation can be produced by remote cues, such as television and newspaper stories
- In extreme cases the affected person fears that he/she will lose his/her own identity and morph into the undesirable personality
- The fear of morphing is sometimes accompanied by a belief that there are contagious germs which can transfer mental instability from person to person
- The affected person feels uniquely threatened
- The person recognizes the irrationality of the fear
- He/she resists the idea
- The person is not delusional
- Usually the person has concurrent or past fears of contact contamination
- In most cases the affected person continues to function at least moderately well
- The fear is accompanied by shame and/or embarrassment
- It impairs the ability to concentrate
- It generates avoidance behavior, mental cleansing, neutralizing, and washing

Case illustrations of different forms of mental contamination

Case 3.1 Physical and psychological violation

Mental pollution was evident in the memories and reactions of a middle-aged patient who had been sexually molested by a relation during childhood. When he recalled the face and the dirty, greasy finger-nails of the perpetrator (a motor mechanic), 30 years after the events, it evoked feelings of dirtiness. "Whenever I remember and imagine his appearance I feel dirty inside. I have to wash myself all over." His childhood fear had evolved into adult fear and loathing. Test probes, in which he was asked to form vivid images of the violator, evoked feelings of inner dirtiness and an urge to shower. He felt dirty all over, and as he was unable to localize the site of the pollution, cleaned his entire body.

Case 3.2 Self-contamination

A puzzled patient developed a fear of certain items of her jewellery and clothing. It transpired that she had worn the contaminated items to church services at one time or another and if she experienced repulsive and blasphemous sexual images during prayers in church, the jewellery and clothes became contaminated. She was tormented by repugnant, uncontrollable thoughts and concluded that she was a hypocrite and secretly subservient to the devil. When her feelings of religious pollution were tackled she made gratifying progress in overcoming the fears of contamination.

Case 3.3 Morphing

A bright and ambitious student experienced an intensive fear that she might somehow "morph" into one of the failing students in her group, and went to lengths to avoid touching or sitting near any of them. If her attempts at avoidance failed, she became distressed and compulsively washed her hands. She spent long hours trying to neutralize the fearful thoughts by internal debates and suppression, but without success.

A financial analyst reported religious obsessions, fears of "ordinary" contamination, and mental pollution. In addition, she described visual contamination, in which she felt contaminated by observing or being in close proximity to people whom she believed were "unlucky" (e.g., a co-worker whom she knew was going to be fired) or who had a "self-destructive personality" (e.g., homeless people). She felt so contaminated by absorbing their undesirable qualities or bad luck that she was compelled to "purify" herself by washing her hands, touching a pure object (e.g., white table), retracing her steps while looking away from the person, or singing a "good" song.

An intelligent young woman feared that she was vulnerable to "mind germs" which emanated from a psychic whom she believed had harmed her by manipulating her mind and her future. After two sessions of fortune-telling, she felt that the psychic had twisted her mind and inadvertently infected her with "mind germs." She regarded the psychic as evil and hated him and anyone else who shared the psychic's name, physical characteristics, style of dress, or accent. The psychic's forecast, she felt, had severely restricted her life, and as a result she fled from the now-contaminated town in which the "infection" had taken place and avoided it, and any reminders of it, for many years. She repeatedly engaged in vigorous and at times frantic compulsive cleaning.

There was no evidence of a delusional disorder in this intelligent and highly educated young woman. Instead her difficulties are best construed as mental pollution. She felt that her mind had been polluted, and the feelings of contamination were easily and daily evoked by mental events such as memories, images, or physical contacts with items/places that had some association with the psychic or the town. Her pollution was not transmissible to other people, had a moral component, and cleaning and intense disinfecting were temporarily relieving but ultimately futile.

An adolescent patient developed a fear of becoming contaminated by physical contact with dirt that gradually expanded into feelings of contamination even when observing at a distance anyone whom she perceived to be dirty. Finally she began to fear that the sight of a dirty person would transform her into a similarly dirty person, and compulsively rubbed her eyes to neutralize the threat. She had no delusions.

"Sleep is my antibiotic for the mind germs." A 35-year-old woman sought treatment for a range of OCD problems, some of which dated back to her adolescence. Raised as a Catholic, she became an agnostic in early adulthood and left the church but was troubled by religious doubts and obsessions. Her feelings of contamination were provoked by contact with any items, places, or people that were associated with germs or pollution, and led to compulsive cleaning. In addition to ordinary contamination, she endured mental contamination that arose without physical contacts. She felt contaminated when she encountered people who were unfortunate, unlucky, or self-destructive (mentally ill, homeless, drug addicted). Even the sight of these people produced feelings of contamination that were virtually identical to those evoked by physical contact with disease/pollution contaminants. The fear that she would acquire their undesirable characteristics and end up in their despairing state was so intense that she even avoided their "airsteam." If she touched them or any of their belongings she was contaminated by what she called their "goof-germs," that is germs which would harm her mentally.

Observing that she was particularly prone to fears of morphing when she was tired, this patient used sleep as a counter tactic—"sleep is my antibiotic." Her account is another example of the belief in the contagiousness of mental instability. She was sure that she was uniquely vulnerable to contamination from the unfortunate strangers, and fully aware of the absurdity of the notion. The patient was gainfully employed and had a successful marriage. She recognized the irrationality of her fears and feelings but was overwhelmed by their power. Her attempts to control the fear were predominantly mental, with an occasional resort to ineffective washing.

Case 3.4 Visual contamination

Victoria developed an intense fear of contamination after being repeatedly humiliated by a colleague who was moved into her work office, and she avoided any contact with the woman or her possessions. The sight of a disabled person also triggered feelings of contamination, visual contamination. Her fear of disability arose from the patient's strong sense of responsibility for the care of her elderly parents. She was an only child and they depended on her for their financial and emotional support. The sight of disabled people, even at a distance, stirred a fear that she might develop a degenerative disease and be confined to a wheelchair, and therefore unable to care for her parents.

A student, Paul, sought help for his fear of being sullied or polluted by visual or physical contact with alcoholics, drug addicts, or louts after being assailed at night by three aggressive men. The sight of such people, even at a considerable distance, distressed him, and if they were too close or particularly troublesome it made him feel so dirty that he had to wash compulsively or take a very hot shower.

Chapter 4

A Cognitive Theory of Contamination Fears and Compulsive Washing

The main premise of *cognitive theories of anxiety* is that disorders develop when a person misappraises the significance of external or internal threats to their health or well-being. The probability and the severity of the threats are seriously overestimated.

The theories are enlightening and constructive, and have moved beyond the early versions that suffered from being too general. The central proposition was applied across the board to all forms of anxiety disorder and was too blunt. The current theories of anxiety disorders start from the main premise and then attempt to explain the specific factors that lead to the development of each of the major types of disorder. All of them are essentially cognitive and are greatly influenced by Clark's (1986) classic example of a specific, and causal, theory to explain panic. The success of Clark's work stimulated attempts to apply Clark's approach to other disorders, and, as a result, new models of social anxiety (Clark and Wells, 1995) and PTSD (Ehlers and Clark, 2000) were formulated. Current theories of OCD focus on the nature and causes of obsessions (Rachman, 1997a, 2003) and compulsive checking (Rachman, 2002), and the present theory tackles a major manifestation of this disorder—the nature and causes of contamination fears and compulsive washing.

Clark (1986) argued that panics are *caused* by a catastrophic misinterpretation of certain bodily sensations. For example, if a person misinterprets his laboured breathing as signifying an impending heart attack, a panic ensues. If it is correctly interpreted as a consequence of climbing stairs too rapidly, no panic occurs. Similarly, Salkovskis's (1985) highly influential cognitive theory of OCD attributes the psychological problems to the person's misappraisal of threat, combined with an inflated sense of responsibility. These two factors are crucially involved in the genesis and maintenance of OCD problems. The cognitive theory of obsessions continues in this line, proposing that obsessions develop and persist if and when a person makes catastrophic misinterpretations of the personal significance of his/her unwanted intrusive thoughts (Rachman, 1997a, 1998). It is timely to apply a cognitive approach to fears of contamination, and the associated compulsive washing.

4.1 What causes mental contamination? A major premise

The cognitive theory postulates that mental contamination is caused by misinterpretations of the personal significance of a physical and/or psychological violation. The source of the violation is invariably a person. The most common violations are degradation, humiliation, painful criticism, betrayal, and sexual assault. Examples of the misinterpretations include a perception that other people regard them as worthless, pathetic, weak, and insignificant. The belief that other people regard one in this way undermines self-confidence and damages the patient's self-appraisal.

Evidence to support the premise comes from an abundance of case histories, many of which are described in this text. Similar case histories in which mental contamination developed after a violation were reported by de Silva and M. Marks. (1999) and by Gershuny et al. (2003) and are described below. In the study by Fairbrother and Rachman (2004) many of the 50 female victims of sexual assault reported intense and persisting feelings of pollution (see Figure 3.1). The laboratory experiments in which the participants were asked to imagine mild violations, such as receiving a non-consensual kiss, produced results showing that personal violations provoke feelings of internal dirtiness in many instances; a significant minority of participants reported urges to wash or gargle (Elliott and Radomsky, 2009; Fairbrother et al., 2005; Herba and Rachman, 2007). Two separate follow-up analyses of these experiments showed that appraisals of personal responsibility and of violation were significant and unique predictors of feelings of contamination—over and above measures of disgust, anxiety, and contamination symptoms (Elliott and Radomsky, 2013; Radomsky and Elliott, 2009). The experimental studies of Coughtrey et al. (2014a,b) on non-clinical participants and on volunteers with diagnosed OCD confirm that feelings of contamination can be induced by recollecting experiences of personal violation such as humiliation and degradation. In therapy, when patients are asked to form a vivid image of a personal violation they usually experience a surge of contamination; typically they report that their feelings of contamination are not confined to their hands but are internal and diffuse, as in the case of Ian (see case illustration in Chapter 1).

The idea that an emotional shock can cause OCD was considered by Janet in 1925. Evidence consistent with the hypothesis that mental contamination develops after physical/psychological violations comes from a number of sources.

This major premise is supported by vivid case histories, the results of laboratory experiments, studies of the reactions to sexual assaults, and the evocation of contamination by asking affected people to recall a particularly troubling experience of humiliation or painful criticism. Sexual assaults are particularly prone to cause mental contamination, and it is notable that sexual assaults are more likely to be followed by mental contamination than are non-sexual assaults, such as being robbed (Badour et al., 2012; de Silva and Marks, 1999; Gershuny et al., 2003). Two of the eight cases of PTSD described by de Silva and Melanie Marks (1999) who developed feelings of contamination were victims of sexual assault, but none of the patients who had been attacked, robbed, or stabbed reported such feelings. Sexual assaults are extremely intrusive and among the most severe instances of a breach of one's personal boundaries.

Immediately after being sexually assaulted while away on holiday, Patient 3 felt "dirty and spent a long time washing herself and everything she had with her at the time. On returning home she continued to feel dirty and said that she could not stop or resist the urge to wash repeatedly." She experienced obsessional thoughts about being dirty and unclean ("I am dirty," "I am filthy," "Everything is unclean") and spent hours washing her body, clothes, and other possessions (de Silva and

M. Marks, 1999, pp. 943–944). The patient recognized that her washing was irrational and excessive but was unable to resist the compulsion or the obsessions. Her initial washing was appropriate, but the feelings of dirtiness and pollution persisted for a long period, as did the associated washing.

The feelings of contamination showed the usual spread from the original source of the dirt/contamination to her clothes and possessions at home. Her feelings of dirtiness were not confined to the affected parts of her body but were general. In addition to feeling dirty after the sexual assault, she experienced mental pollution—pervasive and persistent feelings of internal and external dirtiness, and moral degradation. Intensive washing failed to reduce the unclean feelings or to have any effect on the obsessional thoughts of pollution and filth.

After being raped, Patient 5 developed PTSD and OCD, in which the major symptoms were contamination and compulsive washing. "She felt unclean and washed her hands, body, and home repetitively and in a ritualistic way" (de Silva and M. Marks, p. 944).

Some of the relations between traumatic experiences and feelings of contamination were dissected by Gershuny et al. (2003). Four patients with severe, treatment-resistant OCD and PTSD were treated in a specialized residential facility of the Massachusetts General Hospital. They had undergone horrific trauma and, despite receiving a great deal of treatment (psychodynamic, behavioral, pharmacological), remained seriously disturbed. The connections between their PTSD and feelings of contamination, with associated compulsive washing, are vividly described. One of the patients reported that "trauma-related intrusive thoughts and nightmares immediately triggered obsessions related to cleanliness and a feeling of being 'dirty' which then lead to her showering an excessive number of times throughout the day" (p. 1037).

Another patient described feeling "tainted," contaminated by her thoughts about the violent and sexual trauma she had experienced, and engaged in excessive washing and avoidance. In three of the four cases "some of their contamination fears are not actually related to germs or filth; rather, they seem to feel 'dirty from within' or tainted in some way . . . and such perceptions appear triggered by 'contaminants' even without physical contact to such 'contaminants,'" such as intrusive thoughts and nightmares (p. 1039). During exposure treatment of the OCD, the PTSD symptoms of one patient intensified when direct thoughts regarding her traumatic experiences were evoked (p. 1033).

It is inevitable that many victims of sexual assault feel violated and polluted, and the study reported by Fairbrother and Rachman (2004) confirms that feelings of mental pollution are a common aftermath of sexual assault. Thirty of the 50 students who had suffered a sexual assault endorsed such feelings on a scale devised to assess mental pollution, and there was an association between feeling polluted and excessive washing. For the group as a whole, the deliberate recall of the assault evoked strong feelings of dirtiness, distress, and urges to wash. Recalling a pleasant event produced negligible feelings of dirtiness, but recall of the assault produced a mean dirtiness score of 34/100, a highly significant increase, and 24% of the participants reported strong urges to wash after the recall.

Psychological violation can be a cause of mental contamination. The supporting evidence is abundant case material, including the results of experiments on imagining being the recipient of a non-consensual kiss, the large and immediate effects on OCD patients of forming a vivid image of a personal violation, and the effects of asking OCD patients to recall a significant personal violation. In many cases the feelings of mental contamination have been reduced or removed by therapy in which the violation/s were detoxified.

As described earlier, there is a considerable overlap between mental contamination and contact contamination.

4.1.1 The concept of mental contamination is coherent and measurable

In order to pursue the research program on mental contamination it became necessary to develop scales for measuring the nature and intensity of these feelings. In particular, we constructed a new mental contamination scale to be administered with the Vancouver OC Inventory (VOCI), named the VOCI-MC (see Appendix 2). In extensive psychometric research on clinical and non-clinical samples it was found that the new Scale has one major factor: the items cohere. The concept is measurable and coherent and has high validity (see Toolkit, Appendix 2, for details).

4.2 **Cognitions and contamination**

This distinctiveness of the concept of mental contamination is bolstered by psychometric findings (see Chapter 5) and abundant clinical case material. Feelings of the familiar *contact* contamination are evoked by actual or perceived physical contact with inanimate substances, notably dirt, disease, or dangerous chemicals. Feelings of *mental* contamination are evoked by direct or indirect contact with a person who has violated the sufferer and by cognitions: memories, images, and thoughts that are associated with the violation or violator.

Fear is a response to a perceived threat. The cognitive reactions to threat tend to be similar across all fears, and come down to three possibilities, alone or in combination: a fear of physical harm, a fear of mental harm, a fear of social harm. "I fear that I will get seriously ill, be injured or killed. I fear that I will lose control of my mind/behavior and go crazy. I fear that I will be rejected and isolated from other people."

The threat in fears of disease contamination is clearly enunciated by the affected person. Contact with the contaminant will infect the person and cause serious bodily damage, even death. A fear of the HIV is especially common and is set off by actual or perceived contact with a suspected carrier of the virus or any bodily fluids or possessions of a suspected carrier; blood is a common contaminant. A secondary threat in disease contamination, sometimes even more intense than the fear of harm to oneself, is the threat of being responsible for passing the danger on to other people. The threat of being contaminated by dirt has two elements, an anticipation of disgust and distress, and a secondary dread of the negative social consequences of being dirty or polluted. "I feel polluted/dirty, others can sense it, they will reject and avoid me."

The cognitions associated with external provocations of mental contamination, such as sexual assault, resemble some of the cognitions that are common in PTSD (Ehlers and Clark, 2000). The victims of a personal violation, whether a physical assault or prolonged humiliation, may come to believe that they are irreparably damaged/polluted by the event and that their life is blighted. The very symptoms of their distress, uncontrollable intrusive images, hyperarousal, and irrational feelings of pollution/contamination, reinforce their fears of a dismal future. A feeling of hopelessness is common.

All people experience concern or anxiety if they touch a substance that they believe to be contagious and/or dangerous, and if it is not possible to remove the contaminating material, fear can erupt. However, if the belief is incorrect and/or the perceived threat is exaggerated, the resulting fear is outside the normal range. If the person removes the threatening contaminant, say by a thorough wash, but the perceived threat persists, that too is outside the normal range. A fear of contamination can be abnormally generated and/or abnormally persistent. The root is traceable to a significant, even catastrophic, misinterpretation of the probability of the threatened harm occurring and/or the seriousness of the anticipated harm is grossly overinterpreted.

Fears of contact contamination are less complex than those of mental contamination and invite a single explanation. People fear that physical contact with specifiable contaminants will upset them, threaten their health, and/or compromise their social functioning. In cases of disease contamination, there is a clear connection between the particular contaminant and the feared consequence. In recent years there has been a large rise in fears of contracting AIDS and a steep decline in fears of syphilis. Extreme avoidance of dirt can be driven by a dread of the social consequences of contamination and/or a fear of disease. A fear of mental harm tends to be secondary to the fear of contamination. The abnormally intense level of fear, the dread of spreading the contamination, and the acknowledged irrationality of the compulsive cleansing and avoidance, promote doubts about one's mental stability, and the doubts can be reinforced by the reactions of other people.

4.3 Feelings of contamination and compulsive behavior can be generated and maintained by cognitions

The theory that compulsive behavior, such as compulsive washing, is reinforced precisely because it is successful in reducing anxiety was and is plausible (Rachman and Hodgson, 1980). It helped to validate the rationale for the moderately effective ERP treatment, but recent advances in research on mental contamination show that compulsive behavior can be maintained by *cognitions*.

Clear evidence of the cognitive generation of feelings of contamination, and maintenance of compulsive behavior, comes from the phenomenon of self-contamination. In cases of self-contamination the person's evaluations tend to be self-critical and often have a moral element. "I am impure, sinful, out of control," "I will never get rid of these thoughts and the feelings of contamination," "I can't control my thoughts" (but I should, I must), "I am losing control of my mind." Unwanted, intrusive, repugnant thoughts, images, and urges can induce feelings of pollution. Even though the thoughts are contradicted by the available facts, they remain unyielding and uncontrollable. "These repugnant thoughts and urges, and the associated pollution, are personally significant, and reveal that I have a nasty hidden flaw in my character." Anxiety about losing control of one's thoughts and behavior can generate a dread of becoming mentally unstable, especially as the feelings of internal dirtiness/pollution have irrational qualities, and are exceedingly difficult to control, puzzling, and often repugnant.

For example, thoughts of incest produce feelings of mental contamination—mental/moral pollution and strong feelings of internal dirtiness. The feelings generate a powerful need to remove the dirtiness and usually this takes the form of intensive and repeated washing. The compulsive behavior is maintained by the recurrence of the repugnant thoughts/images. When the images/thoughts are correctly appraised, as in CBT, the compulsive behavior is extinguished. Compulsive behavior is driven by maladaptive cognitions, and the particular form of the compulsion—cleaning, checking, neutralizing—is determined by the specific content of the cognition.

The cognitive generation and maintenance of compulsive washing is also encountered in some cases of *contact* contamination. A young man erroneously believed that he had inadequate control of his bladder and felt that he invariably urinated on himself whenever he took a shower. The faulty cognition generated strong feelings of pollution and he took repeated but unsuccessful showers, a process that commonly lasted

2 hours. The compulsive washing rarely brought relief and often left him more anxious than he had been before starting the washing. His compulsive washing was driven and maintained by recurring cognitions, not by reductions in anxiety.

Why does the compulsive washing persist even when it is less than successful, and why and when does it become compulsive? Washing that successfully removes the contaminant is terminated and therefore presents no problem. Repeated washing that continues for hours, even up to and beyond causing one's hands to bleed, is an ineffective and demeaning compulsion.

The original explanation for the seemingly irrational persistence of futile washing was that the habit of intensive washing continues because it is partially successful; it reduces some anxiety and is therefore functional. The only way to unwind a strongly reinforced habit such as compulsive washing, it was asserted, is to provide the conditions for extinction—repeated but unreinforced evocations of the response. This line of reasoning contributed to the rationale for exposure and response prevention treatment, and is at least partly justifiable. A cognitive explanation is that the fear is preserved because the false belief that the contaminant is dangerous/distressing/morally offensive is shielded from disconfirmation. The affected person seldom or ever learns that the danger/distress/moral element of contamination can diminish without the compulsive washing or be reduced by means other than the compulsive washing.

When the maladaptive cognitions are analysed and modified, the dread of becoming seriously contaminated is reduced. The decline of the fear weakens the urge to carry out the compulsions. Behavior experiments are especially useful for facilitating disconfirmations of the feared threat; disconfirmation of the fear of morphing provides a clear example of this process. Proximity to an "undesirable" person does *not* result in the acquisition of undesirable characteristics or a change in personality. Proximity to a person who has a mental or psychological problem does *not* produce mental instability.

There is, however, a problem with the cognitive explanation. Certain fears are not open to easy disconfirmations, and, in these cases, prolonged persistence of the fear is encountered. The exceptions to the cognitive explanation are fears of contracting a serious illness by contact with a perceived contaminant. It is difficult or even impossible to disconfirm the patient's fear of a future illness, such as AIDS. "If I walk into a hospital I might contract AIDS but won't know it for years because it develops very slowly." In the fear of AIDS, disconfirmations can be obtained by laboratory tests and in many cases do give relief, but unfortunately it fades and the person repeatedly seeks laboratory tests. Moreover, waiting for the results of laboratory tests, which can take 3 months to complete, inflates the anxiety. Commonly, the affected people frequently seek reassurance from the laboratory/clinic and are driven to masking their identity when the clinic/lab staff begin to complain about their annoyingly repetitive requests. The use of exposure therapy in these cases is problematic and some patients decline the treatment because they fear the long-term consequences of being exposed to AIDS-related cues, situations, or discussions. As mentioned earlier, the provision of corrective information about the supposed "contagiousness" of the virus can be ameliorative. The efficacy of ERP exercises is not confirmed.

At present we have laboratory and clinical evidence that feelings of contamination can be generated by cognitions such as thoughts, images, and memories. Laboratory studies of persisting compulsive behavior are limited by ethical and practical considerations, but the available evidence does show that compulsive-like *urges* to wash arise after the induction of mental contamination.

Recognition that compulsive behavior can be generated and maintained by cognitions opens the way for a more comprehensive explanation of this form of abnormal behavior and promotes the development of more tolerable and more effective treatments.

4.4 Why this person, why this fear?

This section addresses two related questions—the vulnerability of affected people, and why there are five different manifestations of mental contamination (e.g. morphing, self-contamination).

In the pursuit of increasingly specific explanations, the outstanding questions are why *this* person and why *this* particular fear? In a series of studies in which undergraduate female students were asked to imagine that they received a non-consensual kiss, many of the participants experienced feelings of pollution/contamination, and a significant minority developed an urge to wash or rinse their mouths (Fairbrother et al., 2005; Rachman, 2006). Mark Boschen (2013) found that imaginal washing was more effective at removing feelings of mental contamination compared to physical washing, atonement, or a waiting period. It has also been found that participants in experiments of this type feel violated and believe that the perpetrator was morally wrong (Elliott and Radomsky, 2013; Radomsky and Elliott, 2009). The reactions to the imaginal non-consensual kiss were influenced by the participants' beliefs/interpretations.

The results of a series of experiments investigating the effects of an imaginal unwanted intrusive non-consensual kiss demonstrated that "mental events," such as images, can induce feelings of contamination and an accompanying urge to clean (Elliott and Radomsky, 2009; Fairbrother et al., 2005; Herba and Rachman, 2007). Coughtrey et al. (2014b) showed that feelings of contamination can also be induced by asking participants to recall a personally humiliating or degrading experience. In a related experiment, induced feelings of contamination were shown to spread to neutral stimuli and to be non-degradable (Coughtrey et al., 2014a).

Just as the content of obsessions is not random (Rachman, 1997a, 1998, 2003), the content of mental contamination is not random. The precise content arises from the particular violation which the affected person endured, and how the person interprets the violation and the actions and characteristics of the violator.

Some people have an elevated sensitivity to contamination, and this in turn is correlated with sensitivities to anxiety and to disgust (see Chapter 5). The postulated sensitivity to contamination is a combination of beliefs/cognitions about the probability and seriousness of threats to one's physical and mental health and a biological reactivity to stimuli that evoke disgust and/or fear. The predisposition is ignited into a fear of contamination by specifiable experiences, for example, sexual assault. The evolution of the disposition into a significant fear occurs as a result of conditioning, observational learning, negative information, or degradation—one or more of the pathways to fear (Rachman, 1990, 2013).

The evidence of a sensitivity to contamination is confirmed by psychometric research (Chapter 5), and the transformation of this proclivity into a clinically significant fear of contamination remains to be investigated.

The particular manifestations of mental contamination make sense in individual cases. As described in Chapter 3, patients who have a weak or uncertain sense of identity are prone to be vulnerable to a fear of morphing, patients who are tormented by repugnant intrusive sexual images or thoughts are prone to develop self-contamination, victims of a serious personal betrayal are prone to develop mental contamination, and so on.

4.4.1 Cognitive biases can generate and maintain mental contamination

Cognitive biases operate in various forms of OCD (Rachman and Shafran, 1998; Shafran and Rachman, 2004), notably in the generation and maintenance of obsessions, but also in generating and maintaining clinically significant feelings of contamination and the associated compulsive behavior. The thought–action fusion (TAF) bias is known to operate in a wide range of conditions, and also in non-clinical populations (Berle and Starcevic, 2005; Shafran and Rachman, 2004; Shafran et al., 1996). The person believes that certain of his or her thoughts can have external effects. The belief that one's thoughts about a possible misfortune actually increase the probability that it will occur is called "likelihood (probability) TAF." The belief that having a morally unacceptable thought is equivalent to an immoral action is called "moral TAF." It is likely that this bias plays a role in self-contamination.

It is also likely that the *ex-consequentia bias* "If I feel anxious there must be a danger," discussed in section 4.3, has a role in mental contamination because of the intensity of the feelings of contamination. As one patient put it, "my hands are aflame with contamination." The feelings are intrusive and tend to dominate other behavior. They are very difficult to ignore and it is a short step to infer that the intense feelings of contamination signal that there is danger.

A new measure was recently developed to assess TAF within the context of contamination fears; the Contamination Thought–Action Fusion Scale (CTAF), which is available in the Toolkit (Appendix 3). It is highly correlated with measures of mental contamination, contact contamination, disgust, and anxiety sensitivity in student samples, but shows less specificity than other measures of cognitive bias (Radomsky et al., 2014).

Activity 4.1: Thought–action fusion (TAF)

TAF is a cognitive bias that often occurs in cases of OCD, and in some other disorders. It can be illustrated, and experienced, by carrying out a simple exercise.

1 Think of a person you are fond of

2 Complete the following sentence by inserting the name of the person in the blank space

3 I think that _____ may twist her/his ankle in the next 24 hours

Some people can complete the sentence easily. Others do so more reluctantly, and some refuse altogether. Why? Reasons such as "bad luck," "bad karma," "what if it did happen?," and "I'd feel terrible" are cited.

After writing it (if you did), do you have an urge to cancel it by inserting the word "NOT" so that it reads _____ will NOT twist her/his ankle in the next 24 hours?" Did you have an urge to call the person to make sure he/she is okay? Did you want to rip up the paper? These are common responses to writing the sentence.

Numerous patients with OCD are prone to TAF, and, after experiencing a disturbing thought or image about harming someone, engage in safety behavior. The thoughts and images can involve fears of contaminating oneself or other people.

The responsibility bias is also observed in OCD—"If I am responsible for preventing a misfortune, that very responsibility increases the *perceived* likelihood that a misfortune will occur." Other examples of the operation of a TAF-contamination bias include these propositions:

"If I have thoughts about getting contaminated, it increases the risk that I will actually become contaminated" and "Having a thought that I might pass on contamination to a child is almost as bad as actually passing it on." The operation of these biases can inflate anxiety and promote compulsive and avoidance behavior.

As mentioned above, TAF probably plays a role in instances of self-contamination. When unwanted intrusive thoughts evoke feelings of self-contamination the TAF bias may come into operation. For example, incestuous images/thoughts are capable of evoking self-contamination and may trigger both types of TAF, the moral and the likelihood biases: "Having these repugnant incestuous thoughts is as immoral as carrying out an immoral action" and "Having violent images increases the probability that I will act in a violent manner." Blasphemous intrusions can trigger moral TAF; for example, a person who has intrusive impulses/thoughts about making obscene remarks and gestures in church interprets the thoughts as the immoral equivalent of committing a sin in church.

Cognitive biases can play a major role in sustaining the feelings of contamination.

4.5 Why do the fears persist?

The main premise of cognitive theories of anxiety is that the affected people significantly misappraise the probability and seriousness of perceived threats. As long as these misappraisals continue, the fear persists. So, why do patients continuously overestimate the probability/seriousness of the threats of contamination despite frequently repeated disconfirmations? This is an important question. They experience the fear of being contaminated hundreds or even thousands of times, but nothing bad happens. In most cases the patient is frightened by perceived contaminants on a daily basis, but no harm ever occurs. In fears of disease-contamination they never catch the dreaded disease.

However, it is not correct to state that "nothing" happens. No disease erupts and no harm is sustained, but the feeling of being contaminated is intrinsically upsetting and alarming. Hence they attempt to remove the source of the discomfort by vigorous washing.

The explanation that washing reduces anxiety is well supported by experiments which showed that anxiety is indeed reduced if the person washes away the contamination (Rachman and Hodgson, 1980), but in retrospect the results were overinterpreted. The results were used to explain why the compulsive *behavior* persists—because it reliably reduces anxiety—but the results did not explain why the *fear* persisted.

In formulating a cognitive construal of compulsive checking, it was necessary to introduce the concept of a self-perpetuating mechanism in order to account for the persistence of the checking (Rachman, 2004). The problem in compulsive checking is similar to the problem encountered in fears of contamination. Why do the patients continue compulsively to check the safety of the house, doors, windows, and stove—thousands and thousands of times—even though no disasters occur? Why does the checking behavior persist despite thousands of disconfirmations? It is possible that a self-perpetuating cycle or mechanism is operating in the maintenance of fears of contamination.

Two forms of cognitive bias contribute to a self-perpetuating cycle which sustains the fear of becoming contaminated. The first bias is the *ex-consequentia* bias, when people infer the presence of danger from their feelings of fear. "If I feel anxious, there must be danger" (Arntz et al., 1995). The idea is that patients engage in "emotional reasoning," i.e., they draw invalid conclusions about a situation on the basis of their emotional response and, most important for the present analysis, infer the presence of danger from their emotional reactions to a potentially contaminating cue or situation.

Encounters with a perceived contaminant evoke anxiety and this is interpreted as a signal of present danger. This resembles the faulty cognition, mentioned earlier, that is expressed in the phrase "It looks clean but feels dirty," and it is experienced in this way—"It looks safe, but *feels* dangerous." The same *ex-consequentia* bias operates in the fear of dirt-contamination. The perceived contaminant evokes strong feelings of fear/disgust and these are interpreted as signaling the presence of significant danger of pollution. This cognitive bias is illustrated in Figure 4.1.

The bias also helps to explain how patients construe their abnormal fear: (i) they are aware that other people do not fear the perceived

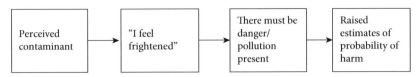

Fig. 4.1 Ex-consequentia appraisals.

contaminant, and (ii) in calm circumstances they know that the contaminant is not truly dangerous. In their fearful moments, however, they feel that they are in danger.

"Yes, it might look safe, but for me it feels very dangerous, and I certainly will not touch it." Talking to a patient about an abnormal thought/fear in a clean, safe, clinical interview room, they usually say, "Yes, it is nonsensical, I know it, but. . . ." In contrast, if you ask the same patient the same question when he or she is inches away from a major contaminant, he/she is decidedly less confident that the fear is baseless. Similarly, a person who is snake-phobic will agree in conversation that garter snakes are harmless but be very frightened if one is brought close to him/her. In calm moments, in the absence of fear, estimations of danger are minimized.

The fear of contamination is regularly evoked whenever the contaminant is encountered. In these circumstances, the arousal of the fear is interpreted to mean that the contaminant is dangerous ("I am frightened so it must be dangerous"). With frequent repetitions, and in cases of contamination-fear this generally means hundreds of repetitions, the patient's estimates of the probability of danger are confirmed and reconfirmed. So, the fear of contamination persists because perception of the contaminant evokes alarm and discomfort, and these reactions are appraised as signifying a threat of danger. The repeated interpretations of fear as signaling a present danger ensure that the person's estimations of probable harm from contamination remain unchanged at a very high level.

The cycle is illustrated by the fear of morphing. "When I see a disreputable or unstable person, I feel frightened—hence, there is danger present. Furthermore, my fear rises steeply as the person comes closer; the danger has increased." "I must escape, I must wash away the danger." In cases of contamination provoked by violation, "When I see the violator my fear rises steeply; there is danger present." Again, "I must escape, and wash away the feeling of danger."

When the *ex-consequentia* cognitive bias is reduced, by therapy and re-education, the overestimations of the probability and seriousness of the threat decline. On the same lines, if the fear reaction to the contaminant is repeatedly weakened, by whatever means (e.g., deep relaxation, tranquilizing drugs), then the inference of danger weakens and the estimated probability of future threats diminishes.

Many patients encounter great difficulty when they attempt to carry out the recommended exposure exercises at home, even though they manage tolerably well in the clinic. They are frustrated when they are unable to repeat the seemingly simple exercises of touching contaminated items at home—even the very items that they have successfully touched in the clinic. "I can't seem to do it on my own; I need someone there with me." In part this difficulty occurs because the patients feel relatively safe in the protected clinic, supported by the staff. They experience less fear, and hence the contaminated items are appraised as less dangerous. In contrast, alone at home their fear is not dampened, and the contaminated items are appraised as very dangerous. The appraised dangerousness of the same item varies in the two sites, except in instances of particularly intense fear. It is moderately dangerous in the clinic, but very dangerous at home.

Returning to the original question of why the fear of contamination persists even though nothing bad ever happens, it turns out that something bad does happen. Rather, two bad things happen, and worse, they happen on every encounter with the perceived contaminant. Similar to the unpleasantness of recurrent episodes of panic, the recurrent episodes of contamination fear are unpleasant (bad event) and the recurrent feeling of being in considerable danger is very unpleasant and unsettling (bad event). One of our patients who had been suffering from OCD for more than 20 years was frightened of dog mess. Originally her fear was based on concerns over illness, but for the past few years she feared the sight of dog mess because she knew that if she saw it, she would need to clean the house excessively for hours. This was a realistic fear. Each encounter with the contaminant strengthens the belief in and the expectation of negative consequences or danger. The original question was baffling because we focused exclusively on the explicit fears expressed by the patients—a fear of contracting a deadly disease, etc. The fears were never realized but still persisted. The cognitive view is that the dread of contamination persists because the feelings of fear are misinterpreted as signaling that there is a threatening unpleasant danger present.

The second, lesser, cognitive bias that enters into the self-perpetuating cycle is TAF. Patients report that having significant, recurrent thoughts about contamination increases the probability that they will actually become contaminated, and also that having contamination thoughts about other people increases the risk that these other people will actually become contaminated. The TAF bias can increase the person's estimations of the probability of harm and the probable seriousness of the anticipated harm. Among patients with an inflated sense of responsibility for preventing harm to others, the TAF bias significantly raises the estimations of contamination-harm, followed by increased guilt and anxiety.

Another self-perpetuating mechanism is the transformation of benign stimuli into triggers (Rachman, 1997a, 1998). According to the cognitive theory of obsessions, a person with a fear of going mad and stabbing someone is likely to become hypervigilant for sharp objects, and this results in sharp objects triggering the intrusive thoughts. Gradually the fear generalizes to more benign objects that resemble the original sharp object, e.g., pens and rulers. Hence when the person comes across a pen or ruler, the obsession is triggered and fear maintained. A similar process operates in mental contamination. Initially the violator is the source of the contamination, the specific trigger, but it can then spread to anyone who resembles that person (e.g., same name, similar clothing, relatives).

Just as repeated compulsive checking causes memory distrust (Radomsky et al., 2006), repeated washing is likely to undermine confidence in one's memory about whether the washing was carried out satisfactorily and fully. These doubts may then maintain the feelings of contamination and contribute to the persistence of the washing. To date there have been no attempts to investigate whether compulsive washing causes memory distrust in a manner akin to compulsive checking.

4.6 **Certain, specifiable memories are contaminating**

Another factor that contributes to the persistence of the fears is memory *enhancement*. In both contact and mental contamination the affected people retain precise and persistent memories of the presence and position of particular contaminants, of potential dangers. In contact contamination the fears are triggered when the person encounters a remembered contaminant. The connections between memories/images/thoughts and feelings of contamination are more direct in cases of mental contamination, and can be evoked at any time, anywhere; this causal connection operates with or without any encounter with a tangible contaminant. Specifiable certain memories can cause feelings of contamination—they are contaminants. Similarly, specifiable intrusive images are contaminants, as illustrated in the case of Ian.

Consequently, patients suffering from mental contamination are exceedingly and lastingly vulnerable. It follows that their vulnerability makes them hypervigilant to memory cues and intrusive images. Memories involving significant contamination experiences are enhanced and long-lasting. As the memories and the intrusive images are *unique* to the affected person, the content of the mental contamination is also unique. As mentioned in section 4.4, just as the contents of obsessions are not random, so the contents of mental contamination are not random. *The qualities of mental contamination are general, but the content is idiosyncratic.*

In his analysis of (emotional) memories, Kahneman (2011) concluded that memories of painful and/or emotional experiences focus on the beginning, peak, and end of the event, to the neglect of the duration of the event. The significant memories of sufferers from mental contamination show the three Kahneman properties, but, unusually, the duration of the feelings of contamination is not neglected. The lengthy unyielding persistence of the feelings of contamination, not infrequently for years, is not overlooked and can be a major cause of despair for the patient.

4.7 **Mislabeling of mood states**

Some patients with OCD misinterpret mood states, such as depression, as feelings of dirtiness. This is similar to the phenomenon in eating disorders where patients can mislabel internal feelings of low mood as feeling "fat." Such patients describe a constant, pervasive, non-localized sense of dirtiness that they find hard to attribute to a specific trigger.

In the treatment of Ian it gradually emerged that contact with items and places contaminated by their association with government letters and agencies distressed him because they induced feelings of sadness and defeat, and not as originally believed because he feared for his health. He "mislabeled" his distressing feelings of sadness and despair as a fear of physical harm—hence his compulsive washing and cleaning was intended to protect his health by maintaining a safe and sterile home.

4.8 **Why is it a current threat?**

Ehlers and Clark (2000) raised the important question of why some people who have undergone a damaging or distressing experience continue to feel under threat for months or years after the precipitating event, but the majority of people do not. Only a minority of people develop a persisting stress disorder after a trauma. Ehlers and Clark recommend that attempts should be made to understand why patients suffering from PTSD continue to feel that they are under serious *current threat*.

The same question arises when considering why only a minority of people develop a persisting fear of contamination, often lasting for many years. Presumably, those people who strenuously avoid contact with a perceived source of infection are under current threat because they fear that contact with the contaminant will produce a serious illness and/or uncontrollable distress. The current threat can spread beyond a fear of incurring damage to one's health or well-being, and expand into a fear of harming other people by passing on the contamination.

In cases of a fear of being contaminated by physical contact with a dirty pollutant, the threat may be to one's health (e.g., contamination from animal or human waste products), but the cases in which it is essentially a fear of dirt as such, for example a fear of greasy feelings, the current threat is not easily evident. There are several possibilities. The person may fear the tension and discomfort produced by touching particular types of dirt, and dread the considerable time, effort, and concentration that will be required in order to carry out the compulsive cleaning. It can take many hours of concentrated effort to complete the process of decontamination. In addition to the dread caused by these two related threats, the uncontrollability of one's abnormal reactions to the contamination can stir a more ominous long-term threat to one's mental stability.

Unfortunately for patients who are afflicted by feelings of mental contamination the dedicated washing and cleaning is ultimately futile. The inability to control their feelings of internal contamination/pollution is a failure that causes distress and contributes to the sense of current threat. They dread the persistence of the unbearable feelings, feel defeated, and resign themselves to uncontrollable pollution and enduring misery.

Similar beliefs are expressed by victims of physical violation who develop feelings of pollution. As in cases of PTSD (Ehlers and Clark, 2000) they may come to believe that they have been permanently damaged, and polluted, by the assault, sexual or physical, and may even abandon the hope of having a normal life. In addition to the general belief that they have suffered irreparable psychological damage, they may also believe that they have been permanently polluted (e.g., Steil et al., 2011). This belief is reinforced by the repeated failures of their dedicated washing. Patients who think that they are vulnerable to a recurrence of the violation become highly vigilant, and any person or cue that is perceived to be polluted or contaminated sustains a sense of current threat.

In cases of a fear of morphing the current threat is that contact with an "undesirable" person will lead to damaging changes in their personality or, in extreme cases, to a loss of identity. There are few fears as fundamental as that of losing one's sense of identity. In cases of self-contamination the cycle of repugnant thoughts/habits leads to compulsive washing, and the current fear is that they are destined to be permanently twisted by their own nature. The primary source of the contamination is always present. The current fear is that they are caught in a distressing psychological problem that is unavoidable, uncontrollable, and chronic. Identification of the patient's current threat is indispensable for formulating a *precise* treatment plan. The main thrust of therapy is directed at removing the current threat, supplemented by whatever means necessary to deal with any remaining fears.

The emphasis on ascertaining the patient's sense of current fear is well justified, but patients' thoughts about their future, a mixture of fears and hope, should not be overlooked.

The evidence to support the hypothesis that people suffering from intense fears of contamination feel under a current threat is indirect and drawn mainly from the convincing work of Ehlers and Clark on PTSD. Our studies of patients suffering from OCD is consistent with their work, but the ultimate value of applying their thinking to understanding the exceptional persistence of fears of contamination requires direct research into the current threats which assail OCD patients. The details of a sense of current threat in patients with OCD, and in mental contamination in particular, need to be collected.

4.9 **Why do fears of contamination ever decline?**

The fear of contamination seldom fades away but instead tends to spread widely and rapidly. Patients will have good days and bad days, but this combination of non-degradability and easy spread of feelings of contamination leads to an expanding net of fears, compulsive behavior, and avoidance. As mentioned earlier, the unchecked feelings of contamination and fear can expand so widely that the person avoids entire cities. There is no spontaneous braking mechanism to prevent the spread of the contamination, and little or no spontaneous decay.

Fortunately the extreme cases of contaminated cities are rare, but the easy spread and non-degradability of contaminants prevail in most cases of the fear. What prevents the ultimate extreme spread of contamination? People oppressed by their feelings of contamination try to control and contain the spread and disabling effects of the contamination by elaborate tactics of avoidance and escape, notably by washing. At best these are exercises in damage limitation. The spread of the contamination can be partly contained by strict avoidance of places and certain people, but this behavior does not reduce the fear. In most instances the contaminants do not degrade, and simply avoiding the contaminants leaves the fear of contamination unchanged. In cases of mental contamination rigorous avoidance of the violator leaves the fear of contamination unchanged, or even increased.

Affected people tend to store the most highly contaminated items in a secure place such as garages or basements. When they finally approach them after many years, as in the course of treatment, they discover that the contamination has not diminished, and may even have increased. Even though the non-degradability of the contamination is most unlikely to be affected by taking medications, some patients find that medications can take the edge off their fear and make life slightly more tolerable.

4.10 **Imagery**

Unwanted intrusive images are common and powerful in OCD (Lipton et al., 2010; Rachman, 2007) and appear to be particularly important in mental contamination. Many patients are tormented by intrusive images of the violator and/or the violation. The images are fully formed, vivid, circumscribed, highly emotional, effortless, and extraordinarily stable. Some images last an entire lifetime.

The identification of contaminating intrusive images is doubly important. It often reveals critical information about the human source of the contamination, and provides the starting point for an effective method of controlling the mental contamination. Unwanted, disturbing intrusive images can be modified/removed by rescripting (see below).

In 1895 Freud made the brilliant observation that "visual memory-images are of course more difficult to disavow than the memory-traces of mere trains of thought" (Breuer and Freud, 1895, 1957 edition, p. 299). As mentioned above, intrusive OCD images are extraordinarily stable. Thoughts evolve, expand, drift, fade, and can be difficult to remember. Freud described patients who disavowed their earlier, significant thoughts: "I may have thought so, but can't seem to remember having done so," (Freud, 1895, 1957 edition, p. 299).

Freud dealt with persistent and resistant images by the so-called talking cure: "A recollection never returns once it has been dealt with; an image that has been 'talked away' is not seen again" (Freud, 1895, 1957 edition, p. 296. This was a remarkably prescient early way of overcoming unwanted intrusive images. It is fascinating that one of Freud's famous cases, Emmy von N., experienced recurrent intrusive images. She had them "very often" and they had the "vividness of reality" (Freud,1895, 1957 edition, pp. 53–55). "My therapy consists in wiping away these pictures, so that she is no longer able to see them before her" and he supported his suggestions to her "by stroking her several times over the eyes." He observed that the "length of time the memory remains in front of the patient's consciousness . . . is in direct proportion to its importance. A picture which refuses to disappear . . . which cannot be dismissed . . . needs to be pursued further." Pictures of little importance are easily dismissed. "Many other hysterical patients have reported to us that they have memories of this kind in vivid visual pictures and that this applied especially to their pathogenic memories" (p. 53).

Incidentally, Freud's observation that pictures of little importance "are easily dismissed" finds an echo in the contemporary cognitive theory of obsessions. Obsessive intrusive thoughts are said to persist if and when the patient attaches great personal significance to the nature of the intruding, unwelcome, repugnant thoughts; intrusions of little personal significance are indeed "easily dismissed" (Rachman, 1997a, 1998, 2003).

The treatment of patients suffering from mental contamination often requires attention to their recurrent intrusive images, and fortunately the straightforward rescripting procedure is a valuable technique for overcoming the distressing intrusions. Moreover, as Beck (1976, pp. 152–157) pointed out, the content of intrusive images can be exceptionally revealing and help to shape the treatment plan.

4.11 Collapse of the fear hierarchy

As with the treatment of other types of fears, contamination fears *collapse downwards*. For example, during exposure treatment a reduction of the fear of a contaminated item that is high on the patient's hierarchy is generally followed by a spontaneous (i.e., non-treated) decline in contamination fears lower down in the hierarchy. Reducing the high level of contamination of an item at the top end of a hierarchy of contaminants can collapse the items lower in the hierarchy. Importantly, this collapse is common during the cognitive treatment of mental contamination.

When the psychological roots of the contamination are identified and modified, the assembly of contamination fears, the hierarchy of fears, tends to collapse spontaneously. It is not necessary to deal with each fear-item in the hierarchy, each contaminated item, separately and independently. The fears of contamination collapse without specific effort, and in synchrony.

In the case of Ian, his extraordinarily large and wide hierarchy of frightening items, people, and places collapsed shortly after he grasped that he was suffering from mental contamination and that washing his hands was futile because his feelings of pollution were internal. A significant change in the patient's appraisal of the human contaminant, and/or a change in appraisal of the seriousness of the threat of the feelings of contamination, leads to a collapse of the hierarchy of fears, and then it is unnecessary to expose the patient to the lengthy list of contaminated items.

The only exceptions to this downward collapse of the fears stem from *categorical* differences. If the patient believes that the non-treated source of contamination is categorically different from the treated source (e.g., my fear of pesticides is completely different from my fear of being contaminated by HIV), a collapse of the fear hierarchy is not likely.

In summary, the evidence to support the cognitive theory consists of abundant clinical material, a series of experiments to test the hypothesis that feelings of pollution and internal dirtiness can be induced by the formation of images of unwanted non-consensual kisses, and recently confirmed by the direct induction of such feelings by asking participants to recall personally humiliating/degrading events.

The non-degradability of feelings of contamination is supported by innumerable cases in which the sufferers continue to experience feelings of contamination for months, years, or decades, and by the laboratory experiments of Coughtrey et al. (2014a) and Tolin et al. (2004).

The research on non-degradability overlaps with the contagion (spread) of contamination.

Studies of the effects of sexual assault show that many victims of these distressing experiences are left with intense and persisting feelings of pollution and contamination. These findings are supported by the laboratory experiments on imagining the effects of receiving a non-consensual kiss. The results of these non-consensual kiss experiments show that feelings of dirtiness and pollution can be provoked by "mental" events, without any physical contact with dirt/disease, etc. It has now been found that when participants are asked to imagine a personally degrading, humiliating event, it can produce feelings of mental contamination (Coughtrey et al., 2014b). Moreover, these feelings are "contagious;" they can easily be transferred to neutral items or objects (Coughtrey et al., 2014a).

The psychometric evidence indicates that the concept of mental contamination is coherent and measurable (Radomsky et al., 2014). Positive progress has been made in testing the effects of the therapy derived from the theory. Many cases have been treated (Chapters 6–10) and a case series was published by Coughtrey et al. (2012b)—see Chapter 11. Full-scale randomized control outcome studies remain to be carried out.

Part 2

Cognitive-Behavioral Treatment of Mental Contamination

Chapter 5

Assessment and Formulation of Mental Contamination

5.1 **The clinical assessment**

Generally, people who are being assessed for possible treatment of a fear of contamination have completed a full psychological evaluation and received a diagnosis of OCD. In deciding whether a course of CBT is advisable clinicians evaluate the contamination/compulsion problem by means of a standardized interview, behavior tests, tests of imagery, and psychometric tests. The assessment consists of the following procedures and usually takes 2–3 hours to complete (see Toolkit for details).

- Standardized Interview for Contamination
- Vancouver Obsessive Compulsive Inventory (VOCI)
- Mental Contamination Scale, appended to the VOCI (VOCI-MC)
- Yale Brown Obsessive Compulsive Scale (YBOCS)
- A detailed account of the present status of the fear and its development
- Assessment of the patient's serious current threats
- Contamination Sensitivity Scale (CSS)
- Contamination Thought–Action Fusion Scale (CTAF)
- Behavior Avoidance Tests
- Recurrent Intrusive Imagery
- Personal Significance Scale (PSS)
  - PSS—Obsessions
  - PSS—Contamination
- Beck Depression Inventory (BDI-II)
- Responsibility Appraisal Questionnaire

Assessments are carried out before, during, and after therapy. The aims of the assessment are to obtain comprehensive information about the patient's fears and compulsive behavior, how the fears and compulsions developed, the responses to previous treatments, and the nature of the current threat. The patient's short-term and medium-term goals are ascertained.

Weekly recordings of the level of fear and any associated washing are collected before each therapy session. In cases of self-contamination and/or morphing, before each session the patient is asked to rate the personal significance which they attach to their unwanted, unacceptable intrusions. The Personal Significance Scale is used for this purpose (Appendix 5). Weekly recordings are associated with improved therapeutic outcome (Lambert et al., 2001).

The Mental Contamination Interview (Appendix 2) is comprehensive. Key features to look for are feelings of contamination with and/ or without a physical contact, a human source/s of the contamination, re-evocation of feelings of contamination by mental events, including images, indications of inner contamination, contamination that is difficult to localize, unresponsive to washing, and the person's *unique* vulnerability to the contaminants. Information is collected about the frequency and intensity of unwanted intrusive thoughts, and compulsive behavior, especially washing.

It is designed to be used flexibly and, as the interview proceeds, some questions are expanded and others omitted, depending on the patient's responses. It covers the following topics: the cues that produce feelings of contamination, the onset of the problem, attempts at coping, washing, and cleaning, avoidance, contamination without contact, sense of internal and/or diffuse dirtiness, evocation of feelings of contamination by mental events such as memories and images, inflated responsibility, feelings of morphing, and proneness to the TAF bias. The complete Schedule is given in Appendix 2 and examples of the questions are shown in Box 5.1.

It is necessary to take a detailed history of the development of mental contamination, including questions about when the problem started, speed of onset, how the patient makes sense of the problem, and personal

Box 5.1 Example questions from the Mental Contamination Interview

- Do some things look clean but feel dirty?
- Do you ever look clean but feel dirty?
- Do you get really bothered by sticky hands?
- Are your feelings of contamination ever set off even without touching a dirty or contaminated object/substance?
- Do you ever feel dirty all over, inside and outside?
- Are your feelings of contamination ever set off by criticism or an upsetting remark?
- Do you ever feel dirty under your skin?
- Do you ever wake up feeling contaminated?
- If you stand close too close to people who look weird or mentally unstable do you worry that you might pick up some of their habits or problems?
- If you think about, and imagine, what caused your feelings of contamination does it make you feel dirty?
- Do you ever feel contaminated after looking at someone who seems to be disreputable, weird, or mentally unstable?
- Is there a particular person or persons who can affect these feelings of dirtiness?
- If you recall what caused the feelings of contamination does it make you feel dirty?

vulnerability. For example, "How do you make sense of the problem?," "If that happened to someone else, do you think they would become contaminated?," "What was happening in your life when the problem first started?," and "What would be the worst outcome?" It can also be helpful to ask for a specific and recent example of mental contamination to elicit thoughts, feelings, and counter-productive behavior (e.g., questions such as "What do you do to cope with your fears?"). Gather information about the source/s of contamination, in particular human sources and hypervigilance to these sources. This includes asking about vulnerability to morphing—"Are you worried you might become like them?" and "How would that happen?"—as well as ascertaining whether the person believed that he/she was able to take on the positive characteristics of a desirable person ("Can you ever pick up positive characteristics?"). A focus on previous or current physical and psychological violations and betrayals is necessary (Rachman, 2010).

This typically begins by asking patients "Can you tell me about anyone who has been particularly helpful to you? What were their characteristics?", before asking them questions such as "Can you tell me about anyone who has been particularly unhelpful to you? You don't have to identify them if you don't wish to. What were their characteristics?".

5.2 **Behavioral assessments**

The behavioral manifestations of a fear of contamination, compulsive washing and extensive avoidance, are so distinctive that they have become emblematic of OCD. From the outset of their work the early behavior therapists recognized the need to record the frequency and intensity of the compulsive behavior and they attempted to assess the behavioral effects of a psychological treatment for this disorder.

The behavior of patients receiving treatment in hospital was monitored by psychologists and nurses, and the patients completed self-recordings. The collection of behavioral self-recordings from out-patients depended on the person's cooperation and conscientiousness, but in practice this information was incomplete and sometimes of doubtful accuracy. The introduction of behavioral avoidance tests, consistent with Lang's (1985) clarifying construal of fear, was a simple, useful step forward. He introduced a test in which snake-fearful participants were asked to walk towards a live snake and report their fear on a 0–10 scale at each point of the approach. The main measures were the closeness of the approach to the snake and their fear ratings. These tests were administered before and after desensitization therapy and at a follow-up. The method was widely adopted and remains an important measure of change in OCD, especially in cases of contamination fear.

In addition to behavior and verbal reports, Lang recommended the use of psychophysiological measurements. They are employed in research projects but not used routinely during cognitive therapy for contamination fears. On occasions, simple measures such as pulse-rate can be useful if the patient is perplexed about the source, content, and site of their feelings of pollution and contamination. They are also useful when testing the effects of recurrent, distressing intrusive images.

Behavior experiments are used in CBT predominantly as a method for encouraging patients to collect direct, personal information that is pertinent to their cognitions about contamination. For example, they can be used to ascertain whether the patient feels contaminated by the sight of "undesirable" people, and if so, which people. The experiments are also valuable in treatment.

Behavior experiments are carried out to collect fresh information and are generally one-offs. It is best to avoid confusing them with exposure therapy sessions, which are conducted repeatedly and for prolonged periods in order to evoke the fears in an attempt to "habituate" the patient's reactions to the fear stimuli. Unlike behavior experiments, exposure treatments invariably include response prevention.

5.3 **Intrusive images**

As observed by Beck (1976), and earlier by Breuer and Freud (1895, 1957 edition, pp. 53–55), intrusive images can be exceptionally revealing. In the case of Ian described in Chapter 1, when he formed an intrusive image of a degrading event it made him feel intensely contaminated within less than a minute. He was contaminated "all over," internally and on his skin. This reaction revealed to him that his feelings of contamination were instantly evocable by personal images, without touching any tangible contaminant. The prevalence and power of unwanted intrusive images in OCD is so diagnostically and therapeutically significant that test probes of these images are an important part of the assessment procedure (Rachman, 2007).

After discussion of the patient's experience of intrusive images, a few neutral and a few sensitive examples are assembled and then examined by *test probes*. After establishing a baseline level of contamination, the therapist asks the patient to form vivid, realistic images involving the person or situations which feature in their naturally occurring images, such as the primary source of mental contamination—the violator.

These are some examples. Ask patients to report the degree of contamination they are feeling at present on a 0–100% scale that ranges from none at all (0%) to the maximum (100%), then ask them to form a clear, realistic image of the violator. The patients indicate by a hand signal when they have formed the image, and are asked to hold the vivid image for approximately 2 minutes and then report any feelings of contamination or dirtiness and any urges to wash. The second test follows the same pattern—baseline, then image, then self-report—and this image can be the "violator" touching the patient. The third test can involve an image of the patient handling a significant possession of the violator, e.g., clothing. A fourth test is imagining sharing a drinking glass with the violator.

The patient reports any feelings of contamination, the location of the feelings, any urges to wash, and any negative emotions such as disgust or anxiety. Images that evoke significant contamination are rescripted into preferred images that the patient selects.

Once they have acquired the method, patients are encouraged to rescript any nasty images that arise, as necessary. Often this is very successful and gives the patients a sense of control as well as relief from distress.

Some patients describe imaginary shields they have developed to protect themselves from contamination. It can be helpful to ask "Do you ever take unusual steps to protect yourself?".

5.4 **Psychometrics**

The early psychometric scales, such as the widely used Maudsley Obsessional Compulsive Inventory (MOCI), were constructed during the behavioral era, and virtually all of the items addressed observable behavior (Hodgson and Rachman, 1977). The scale established the existence of two major factors, checking compulsions and cleaning compulsions, which mirrored the most common clinical manifestations of OCD. The major findings were replicated in related scales, but when the limitations of a narrowly behavioral approach became apparent, a revised expanded MOCI scale, the VOCI, was developed. It has a wider range of items and includes essential cognitive items (Thordarson et al., 2004). It has excellent psychometric properties in both student and clinical populations (Radomsky et al., 2006). The change from a subscale that measures compulsive washing (MOCI) to a subscale that measures fear of *contamination* (VOCI) is an improvement that provides a tool for more precise investigations of the two phenomena.

As the concept of contamination was expanded and elaborated, the VOCI scale was introduced and two contamination elements are now included (the *contact contamination subscale* and *mental contamination scale*, see below). The earlier tests, from the MOCI onwards, were based on the prevailing view of contamination, namely that all contamination arises from physical contact with a contaminant. In order to carry out investigations of mental contamination, the VOCI contamination subscale is supplemented by measures that collect information about mental pollution, self-contamination, and morphing. The Mental Contamination Interview of the VOCI, provided in Appendix 2, was the strongest predictor of self-reported dirtiness and urge to wash among the "contaminated" participants in the Herba (2005) replication experiment.

In order to advance our understanding of the cognitive underpinnings of mental contamination, three new measures were developed (Radomsky et al., 2014). The contents of the new measures were based on the theory described earlier (see also Rachman, 2006) and on descriptions provided by patients and clients of the nature of their perceived "contaminants," as well as clinical observations. The CSS (see Appendix 4) is designed to assess the degree to which people become distressed or upset by their feelings of contamination, e.g., "It scares me when I feel dirty *inside* my body." Finally, the CTAF (see Appendix 3) was developed to assess the possibie fusion between thoughts about contamination and feelings and behavior associated with contamination, building further on the construct of TAF (Shafran et al., 1996), e.g., "If I get an image of myself being contaminated, it will make me feel contaminated."

The three new measures have excellent internal consistency across four groups of participants (those with OCD in which contamination fear was evident, those with OCD in which no contamination fear was evident, those with an anxiety disorder other than OCD, and student controls; Radomsky et al., 2014). Among those in the OCD Contamination, OCD Non-Contamination, Anxious Control, and Student Control groups, Cronbach's Alphas for the VOCI-MC were 0.94, 0.97, 0.96, and 0.93 respectively; for the CSS these were 0.90, 0.94, 0.91, and 0.92 respectively; and for the CTAF these were 0.96, 0.96, 0.95, and 0.93 respectively.

In general, there were strong and significant correlations between the VOCI-MC and the CSS in all groups, with weaker associations between the CTAF and CSS (Radomsky et al., 2014). Two of the three new scales were strongly and significantly correlated with the Contamination Subscale of the VOCI across all three groups; the VOCI Contamination Subscale–CTAF correlations in the two clinical groups were not significant. With some minor exceptions, correlations between the three new mental contamination scales and the BDI (Beck et al., 1996) were lower (and, in many cases, substantially lower) than those with VOCI Contamination Subscale scores across all groups of participants. Importantly, the VOCI-MC and CSS successfully discriminated between those with OCD who reported contamination-related concerns and all other groups of participants tested in the study. The CTAF discriminated only between clinical and non-clinical groups. Particularly strong relationships emerged between the VOCI-MC and VOCI total ($r = 0.78$) and VOCI Contamination ($r = 0.70$) scores, between the CSS and VOCI Contamination ($r = 0.74$) scores, and between the CTAF and TAF ($r = 0.74$) scores. In terms of beliefs, the Obsessive Beliefs Questionnaire (OBQ) (Obsessive Compulsive Cognitions Working Group, 2003) Responsibility/Threat and OBQ Importance/Control over Thoughts beliefs were significantly correlated with each new mental contamination scale, whereas only the VOCI-MC was significantly correlated with beliefs about Perfectionism/Intolerance for Uncertainty as measured by the OBQ.

These findings have a number of important implications for our understanding of contamination in general and mental contamination in particular. The results demonstrate that mental contamination is a coherent and readily measurable concept. Previous measures of contamination (e.g., the VOCI, OCI, YBOCS) have focused exclusively on contact contamination and overlooked mental contamination.

The ability of the VOCI-MC and CSS to discriminate between people who report symptoms consistent with contamination-based OCD and those who had other forms of OCD is particularly welcome and useful. Its specificity allows clinicians to distinguish between contamination-related OCD and other forms of this heterogeneous disorder, although more information is needed about the assessment of mental contamination in other disorders (e.g., PTSD). It is unsurprising that CTAF does not have this degree of specificity; the construct of TAF itself is not specific to OCD but occurs across a wide range of anxiety disorders (Abramowitz et al., 2003), and this appears to be true as well for the more specific CTAF.

The clinical cut-off score for the Mental Contamination Scale is 39 (Appendix 2).

Unlike earlier tests of OCD, the VOCI-MC is not blurred by strong associations with general distress, especially depression and anxiety. The "purity" of this simple VOCI-MC, if confirmed, will help clinicians to identify a problem that warrants therapeutic priority—mental contamination.

The three new scales (with emphasis on the VOCI-MC) demonstrated an encouraging ability to predict unique variance in OCD symptomatology over and above anxiety, depression, anxiety sensitivity, disgust sensitivity, OCD beliefs, TAF, and traditional contact contamination symptoms among patients diagnosed with OCD, and among student controls (Radomsky et al., 2014). Although the amount of variance predicted was small (i.e., 2.4% in the student sample, 3.5% in the OCD sample), it supports the idea that the new measures capture an important and meaningful element not previously identified in standard OCD self-report scales. The original VOCI captures established domains of symptomatology (e.g., checking, obsessions) and characteristics and features of OCD which tend not to be assessed by other standard OCD measures (e.g., hoarding, "just right" symptoms, indecisiveness). The new mental contamination measures are robust predictors, over and above a number of regularly used measures of OCD beliefs, depression, and anxiety, and lead us to recommend their use, especially of the VOCI-MC, in both research and clinical applications in which contamination-related phenomenology is of interest.

The strong relationships seen between the three new measures and other OCD-relevant symptoms and constructs are indicative of the degree to which mental contamination is often interwoven with other aspects of OCD, although it remains to be seen how they line up with measures of other problems and pathologies. The strong relationships between these three new measures and contact contamination are not surprising; but robust correlations with "just right" symptoms, obsessions, responsibility, the importance of/control over thoughts, and TAF highlight a number of domains worthy of future study.

For some time, the term "compulsive washing" has been used interchangeably with the fear of contamination. However, the two terms and concepts should be distinguished. Not all people with elevated fears of contamination engage in compulsive washing but neutralize their fears idiosyncratically (e.g., by swallowing water, by praying for spiritual purity, or by constructing a mental shield; Coughtrey et al., 2013b). Similarly, some people engage in compulsive washing not because they fear contamination but because they don't "feel right."

Further research on the mental contamination scales is required to consolidate their specificity and sensitivity and determine whether they can be used as a reliable measure of therapeutic change. In successfully treated cases the VOCI-MC tends to plummet from very high levels to well below clinical levels. Examinations of relationships between the new measures and treatment status, disorder duration, and/or with alternate measures of severity may well be useful. In addition, their inclusion in studies of contamination-related phenomenology is recommended. The scales are in the Toolkit and are available for public use free of charge from any of the authors. See Box 5.2.

5.5 Formulation

An individualized formulation of the maintenance of the problem is devised, based on the theory of mental contamination (Rachman, 2006). The formulation is focused on triggers of mental contamination (including imagery), beliefs relating to contamination, and maintaining

Box 5.2 Conclusions from the psychometric data

- Contamination is a coherent concept, and is measurable
- In all scales designed to measure OCD, contamination/compulsive cleaning and compulsive checking emerge as the major factors
- Mental contamination scales meet the standards for reliability and validity
- Mental contamination scale scores are associated with clinical manifestations of fear of contamination, and with compulsive cleaning
- Contamination/washing subscales are modestly, and appropriately, correlated with other OCD subscales, such as obsessions and checking, but not with hoarding and slowness
- In some recent scales the term has been changed from compulsive washing to *contamination*
- The indications are that the VOCI-MC is satisfactorily specific
- Unlike other tests of OCD, the VOCI-MC Scale is not blurred by associations with general distress, especially depression and anxiety. The "purity" of the mental contamination scale, if confirmed, will be an advantage in future research
- Measures of mental contamination predict unique variance in OCD symptoms, over and above measures of general distress, contact contamination, and OCD beliefs
- In future psychometric and other research a distinction should be made between the fear of contamination and compulsive washing. The two terms should be distinguished, and so should the two concepts
- The sensitivity and reliability of the VOCI, and especially the Mental Contamination Scale, as measures of therapeutic change, remain to be determined

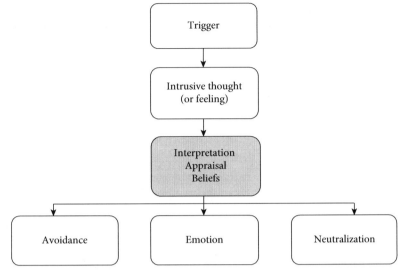

Fig. 5.1 A cognitive-behavioral model of OCD.

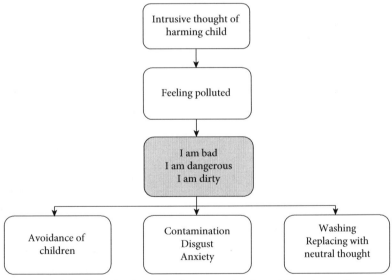

Fig. 5.2 A cognitive-behavioral model of an example of mental contamination.

behavior (e.g., compulsive washing and avoidance) (see Figure 5.1 and Figure 5.2). It illustrates the self-perpetuating nature of the problem and is adapted from the classic construal of the maintenance of OCD. For more general information on the collaborative nature of case formulations and how to build one, see Kuyken et al. (2009).

Chapter 6

Overview of Cognitive Behavioral Treatment of Mental Contamination

Recognition of the disorder of mental contamination necessitated the development of new methods of treatment. It is essentially a cognitive disorder and therefore a cognitive form of treatment is appropriate. Given the cognitive theory of anxiety disorders, and the specific cognitive theory of OCD, the primary aim of therapy is to assist patients reduce their serious misinterpretations of perceived serious current threats. Specifically, the aim is to reduce their significant overestimations of the probability and seriousness of the threats, as observed in the benefits experienced by the many treated cases of mental contamination and illustrated in the experimental investigation of the therapeutic effects of reducing the sense of danger (Vos et al., 2012). In particular cases the cognitive methods are integrated with ERP, as necessary.

Mental contamination is a major factor in roughly 50% of patients with OCD with abnormally elevated feelings of contamination. In 33% of these there is an overlap between mental contamination and contact contamination. In the majority of such cases the best way to proceed is to tackle the mental contamination first because it is common for a significant reduction of the mental contamination to be followed by a weakening or even disappearance of the contact contamination, as in the case of Ian. The hierarchy of frightening contaminants collapses.

Tackling the contact contamination first, usually by ERP, can be insufficient. Very many of our patients with mental contamination had already had one or several courses of ERP treatment directed at the contact contamination, including Ian described in Chapter 1, and benefitted from some initial improvement but then experienced a return of fear.

After a very welcome amelioration of their fears of contamination, the improvements tended to fade and left them with significant fears of contamination that were evoked *without physical contact* (images, thoughts, memories). Eleven percent of our OCD patients had 'pure' contact contamination fear, and in these cases ERP is recommended.

The treatment of mental contamination comprises two parts. The initial part consists of discussions of corrective information, the patients' appraisals of their contamination, and a description of the procedures for treating mental contamination. The second part consists of specific procedures that are designed to deal with the diverse manifestations of the contamination. These are used in treating the five forms of the phenomena (morphing, self-contamination, etc.) described in Chapter 3.

The treatment focuses on the primary source of the contamination—a significant person in the patient's life (violator). Therapy sessions concentrate on the characteristics and history of the violator and the circumstances in which the contamination arose (e.g., degradation, betrayal, humiliation). The patient's current appraisals of the violator and the violations are discussed in detail and analysed.

The reasons why the person feels under *current threat* are considered, and the evidence to support or disconfirm the person's appraisals is assembled. The intention is to assist the patient to develop an alternative, adaptive, realistic appraisal of the current threat. Much of the therapy is concerned with the patient's prevailing feelings of contamination and the question of why the feelings have persisted for so long after the critical events—often, long after contact with the violator has ended. *The feelings of contamination can persist even after the violator has died.*

In the early stages of therapy some patients are perplexed by the therapist's interest in seemingly unrelated and even remote "mental events." They may question the relevance of these events to their fear of contamination and their compulsion to wash repeatedly and vigorously. As one patient expressed it, "How on earth can my fiancee's betrayal have anything to with my fear of becoming contaminated when I touch my own clothing?" A pertinent question.

The therapy sessions tend to be complex, concentrated, and so busy that patients and therapists can benefit from listening to the complete recording or the parts that appear to be especially significant. It is advisable to record all sessions and provide patients with a copy of the recording at the completion of each session if they so wish. These serve the triple purpose of fostering the processing of session material, of sending the recorded sessions and information "home" for review and interpretation, and also as an archive of therapy sessions during and after the programme of therapy.

6.1 General procedures

The nature of OCD and fears of contamination is discussed and patients are given printed material that includes an outline of the CBT (see Toolkit). The aim of the treatment is to help patients modify their unadaptive cognitive misinterpretations/beliefs about the personal significance of their fear of contamination. Therapy consists of cognitive analyses and cognitive techniques for modifying the maladaptive interpretations.

6.2 Psycho-education

A semi-didactic component to provide psychological-education and corrective information (Rees et al., 2013) about mental contamination is included. Patients are asked what they know about OCD and contamination fears. The different types of contamination are described, including descriptions given by previous patients: "There is another kind of contamination in which people experience very similar feelings [to contact contamination] like feeling dirty or polluted but without touching anything. This kind of contamination is not localized to your hands but is diffuse. It can be a sense of internal dirtiness, within the body, or spread all over your body. These feelings of internal dirtiness or pollution are not uncommon. Some people describe it like having 'mind germs' because certain thoughts and images can convey the feeling of contamination." The purpose of the semi-didactic component is to normalize patients' fears and provide assurance that such experiences are not a sign of impending doom. Morphing fears are particularly prone to be interpreted as indicative that the client is going mad. Patients with a fear of morphing may have been told by friends, relatives, or professionals that their thoughts mean they are mentally ill.

The human source of mental contamination is explained: "Mental contamination invariably starts from a person/s. People who are afflicted with mental contamination have sometimes experienced physical or emotional violation, for example, being degraded, humiliated, by a betrayal, domination by a parent, or an assault—and this can sensitize them to fears of contamination. The fears can spread and generalize by becoming associated with particular categories of people."

The role of concealment in maintaining appraisals is described. A further area for discussion is mislabeling mood states, separating feelings of anger, aversion, and disgust from feelings of mental contamination, and explaining the ex-consequentia reasoning bias to clients (e.g., "Some people reason that if they feel guilty, they must have done something wrong and therefore they think, 'I am contaminated.' Sometimes when people think they are feeling dirty or polluted they are actually also feeling sad or angry or disgusted but have mislabeled the emotion, and that's why washing doesn't help you feel better.").

The psychological treatment for OCD is CBT. Generally it takes about 12 one-hour sessions of individual therapy, with an interval of a week or so between sessions. In this therapy the nature and development of the OCD is traced and analysed and particular attention is given to the reasons why the patient currently feels under serious threat. The next step is to provide corrective information and carry out various therapeutic exercises.

Non-technical books, including self-help books, that provide comprehensive descriptions of the CBT in general and psychological treatment of all the various manifestations of this complex disorder can be useful (see Shafran et al., 2013). The present description deals with fears of contamination and the consequent compulsive behavior, especially repetitive intensive washing and cleaning. Feelings of contamination can be extremely intense, demanding, and distressing and generate overwhelming urges to get rid of the contamination.

It is explained that there are two forms of contamination fears. The familiar form, in which the feelings of contamination arise after touching a dirty/disgusting/dangerous object or item that is tangible (such as a discarded dirty bandage) is called *contact contamination*. The other form, *mental contamination*, develops when a person is psychologically/emotionally or physically violated by another person. The feelings can be caused by a sexual assault or intensely humiliating or degrading experiences such as a betrayal and are easily evoked by disturbing memories, images, remarks, or insults—or anything or anyone associated with the violator. Unlike contact contamination this form of contamination can arise and be re-evoked without any physical contact with dirty or disgusting tangible objects. The source of mental contamination is always a person, not an inanimate object.

The prevailing treatment of *contact contamination* involves repeated and prolonged exposures to the full range of contaminating stimuli. During and after the exposures, patients are firmly encouraged to refrain from carrying out any cleaning or washing. This exposure treatment (ERP) is demanding but at least moderately effective. It can be uncomfortable because the aim is to ensure that every exposure to the contaminating stimuli evokes anxiety, and that the person endures it. The expectation is that with frequent repetitions of the exposures the patient will gradually become accustomed to contacts with the contaminant. The insistence on response prevention is not always necessary (Rachman et al., 2011).

CBT helps patients to reinterpret their maladaptive thoughts of serious harm coming from physical or non-physical contact with the contaminants. Two possible explanations of their fearful expectations are developed; the first is benign and the second is threatening. Evidence that supports the alternatives is collected by discussions, analyses, image rescripting, and behavior tests. When the patient concludes that the benign alternative is best supported by the evidence, the fear declines or disappears.

Usually the therapist will have an account of the patient's problem from the referring source, supplemented by the results of psychological tests. If the presence of mental contamination is probable, a course of

CBT is recommended. The initial sessions are devoted to tracing the development of the disorder, and given that the patient will have experienced a significant physical or psychological violation, describing and talking about the people involved and the events that occurred tends to be highly emotional. Hence, a gentle gradual therapeutic approach is used, with emphasis in the early sessions on fostering an understanding and supportive therapeutic alliance.

As the therapy proceeds, specific techniques are introduced. These include the modification of distressing, recurrent, unwanted images (pictures in the mind), testing out new ways of overcoming the unadaptive avoidance that accompanies this disorder, helping the patient to appraise the people who have had a major effect on their lives—such as the violator/s and also people who have been particularly kind, supportive, and helpful.

As well as providing psycho-education, it can be worthwhile discussing the problem and progress with family members because the affected people can be misunderstood by people who are puzzled why they wash their hands intensively even though they haven't touched any of the designated contaminants. The psychological-education also helps to explain why one wash is seldom sufficient. "The perceived contamination is not circumscribed, is not limited to hands. Hence giving your hands a thorough wash fails to help, and perhaps you try washing again, even more thoroughly. Feelings of contamination that are set off by a memory, or image, or thought, tend to persist even after a thorough wash—regardless of the clean state of your hands."

6.3 **Monitoring**

Clients are asked to monitor and record contaminating triggers (in particular, human sources and their own thoughts and images), the intensity of mental contamination, location of pollution within themselves, and subsequent behavior (e.g., forming a protective image, avoidance, washing, drinking water). Personalized session-by-session monitoring of symptoms is utilized throughout treatment (e.g., recording the frequency and intensity of contaminating and protective images).

Self-monitoring is used to increase a patient's general understanding and insight into mental contamination. It is distinct from session-by-session monitoring, which is used to assess symptoms on a regular basis and is also recommended. With self-monitoring, patients can be helped to pay attention to, or monitor, particular cognitions, emotions, or behavior associated with feelings of mental contamination. Many therapists ask their clients to engage in self-monitoring but then give up when their clients come back saying they didn't monitor. However, research evidence shows that some people can make significant improvements from simply monitoring their symptoms. For example, Ehlers and colleagues (2003) found that 12% of people with PTSD symptoms following a traffic accident recovered sufficiently after 3 weeks of daily monitoring of their intrusions, and no longer met diagnostic criteria for PTSD.

6.4 Surveys

Surveys are used to collect personally relevant information relating to mental contamination. In some cases this is used to normalize the fears, as with traditional CBT for obsessions—for instance, by asking friends/relatives how they would feel about wearing the clothing of someone who has died. In other cases a survey can be related to more specific concerns such as moral standards, reaction to particular categories of people, or ways of coping with emotions such as guilt and depression. Surveys are widely used in CBT for OCD (e.g., Whittal et al., 2010). They were originally used to help patients learn that everyone experiences unwanted intrusive thoughts, based on the work of Rachman and de Silva (1978). In the treatment of mental contamination, they are used primarily for information-gathering about standards, beliefs, behavior, and emotions held by other people. Some information may be easily available, but conducting a survey allows the patient to gather *personally relevant* information from people whose opinion they respect or whose opinion is particularly pertinent. The fear of moral transgression that is so characteristic of mental contamination reflects the personal values held by patients. Having information about how highly moral people who are not crippled by

OCD manage to live happy lives can be extremely helpful. Such surveys can also help "set the bar" for the relevant concern, e.g., morality, handwashing.

No two surveys are exactly alike. The survey you and your patient collaboratively construct will vary depending on the sort of area in which the mental contamination is being expressed.

The key to constructing a survey is to ensure that it has personal relevance and meaning, so that the information gathered has high evidential value. Surveys are mostly written, but we have used images in the past for a client. Sometimes patients are reluctant to engage in surveys as they are concerned about directly asking others or that others might know it is about their beliefs. In this case, anonymous surveys using electronic software may be helpful.

6.5 **What to do with the information from surveys**

1 *Collect the responses*

The survey responses should be the first item on the agenda (or the second item, right after reviewing the patient's monitoring). Having the responses laid out in front of you on the table so you can work through them together can be particularly helpful.

2 *Draw conclusions*

Going through the responses together, the goal is to help the patient reach conclusions about where other people set the standard, or the impact of the survey on the patient's beliefs about mental contamination (e.g., whether it can spread or not). Making a summary table or graph of the information can be clarifying. It is likely there will be a range of responses and this variability can help the client recognize that there is no absolute "right" and "wrong."

3 *Check reality*

Many clinicians are concerned about doing surveys in case the responses are unhelpful. For example, if you ask someone about their moral standards, they might be excessively high. However, if you have chosen a reasonable number of people, then the reaction of them all—including the variability—will provide useful information.

4 *Follow up alternative beliefs*

Surveys, like monitoring and psycho-education, will help the client formulate alternative beliefs. It is highly unlikely that formulation of alternative beliefs will be sufficient for cognitive or behavioral change. Following up the generation of alternative beliefs with behavioral experiments is helpful in facilitating a new and more benign perspective in the long term.

Each survey is idiosyncratic and discussion of the meaning of the results in detail is a priority for the therapy session. Surveys can help facilitate the generation of an alternative belief that should then be further evaluated using some of the cognitive strategies and behavioral experiments described in the next chapters.

6.6 Changing the meaning of mental contamination by tackling beliefs and biases

Much attention is paid to the personal significance which the patient places on the cognitions, and the process is facilitated by using the Personal Significance Scale (PSS) (see Appendix 5). The Scale serves two functions: it is a diagnostic measure and a process measure.

It is used to monitor the personal significance which the patient attaches to his/her feelings of contamination (e.g., "The feelings make me feel mentally unstable, out of control, weak, in imminent danger") and enables the therapist to monitor progress. All proceeding well, as the patient moves towards a realistic and acceptable evaluation of the meaning of the feelings, the scores on the PSS decline.

If a patient's weekly scores on the PSS do not decline, the treatment plan needs to be reviewed. If a successfully treated patient experiences a return of fear and compulsions the PSS scores will show whether the original misappraisals have returned or whether some new cognitive misappraisal has developed. The PSS often is used in collaboration with the analysis of competing explanations—Explanation A vs. Explanation B.

6.6.1 **Explanation A vs. B**

A useful method for evaluating the patient's maladaptive beliefs is the procedure known as "contrasting explanations." It involves the assembly of the patient's reasons that support his or her anxious cognitions. The patient and therapist formulate two possible explanations of the problem. For example, theory A is that "my mental contamination is a form of illness and not controllable" and theory B is that "mental contamination is a recognizable psychological problem that can be dealt with by therapy." The contrasting explanations are evaluated by discussions of the available evidence supplemented by any fresh evidence collected during behavioral experiments. The experiments give patients an opportunity to collect direct personal information pertaining to their key cognitions; the evidential value of direct information exceeds statistical information, therapist's accounts, second-hand accounts of the experiences of other people, or information found on the internet. In some cases, the patient has more than two explanations, but the assembly and evaluation of each proceeds as it does for two competing explanations.

Evidence for and against the patient's two explanations is assembled and evaluated systematically. When necessary, new information is gathered by behavior experiments, personal surveys, and evocation of distressing/troubling images.

6.6.2 **Responsibility appraisals**

If a patient returns an elevated score on the Responsibility Appraisal Questionnaire (Appendix 5) therapy is provided as needed. Elevated levels of responsibility often exacerbate and maintain feelings of contamination. The person's appraisals of his or her responsibility are analysed in a pie chart, which usually reveals obvious imbalances and implies the need to reduce and shift responsibility. Progress in reducing excessive responsibility is assessed by repeat administrations of the pie chart.

To start the pie-chart exercise, it is helpful to ask patients how responsible they feel (in percentage terms) for protecting themselves and/or others from danger (often in the form of perceived contaminants, but sometimes from a particular person). At this initial stage, most patients indicate very high levels of perceived responsibility (e.g., 80–100%). This is then illustrated in a pie chart, showing that nearly all of the "pie" is taken up by the patient's own responsibility. The therapist then engages the patient in discussions of many/all of the other people or groups who have some responsibility for averting harm/danger. This list often includes family members, friends, co-workers, public employees (e.g., hospital workers, janitorial staff), and other people (e.g., supermarket employees, strangers, manufacturers of cleaning products). Once a moderate number of people/items are listed (somewhere between 5 and 20), the therapist works with the patient to allocate percentages of responsibility to each person or group on the list. When this is complete, a new pie chart is drawn up reflecting the revised allocation of responsibility across multiple individuals. The amount that cannot be allocated to others is then left to the patient. This amount is unlikely to be zero but is almost assuredly going to be less than the initial amount described above. Patients are encouraged to share the responsibility with others and to remember that others are continually playing a role in keeping things clean and safe. Often, the revised pie chart is sent home with the patient, who might be encouraged to generate another chart, perhaps for a different situation.

One client who contracted food poisoning while dining at her mother-in-law's home felt that since her mother-in-law hadn't acted responsibly, she needed to take responsibility for ensuring that all food was clean and safe for her, her husband, and their small child. Over time, this initially contact-based contamination generalized and the now-mental contamination-related problems include repeatedly washing anything that might have been associated with her in-laws (through contact, imagery, or even discussion). The patient assessed her responsibility for protecting her family to be 98%, but the pie-chart exercise helped her to reallocate responsibility to her husband, her nanny, grocery store employees, and her father-in-law (but not, at least initially, her mother-in-law). When the new pie chart was drawn out showing only 35% remaining for the patient, she expressed relief and, as a behavioral experiment, tried living with only 35%

responsibility as far as all perceived contaminants (mental and physical) were concerned. The following week, she reported substantial
(albeit incomplete) declines in her fears of contamination and associated washing behavior.

6.6.3 Cognitive biases

The universality of unwanted intrusive thoughts and the operation
of cognitive biases such as TAF, and the *ex-consequentia* bias, are
explained. "Your fear reaction when you see a contaminant has become
a very strong habit, but that feeling of fear does *not* mean that you are
actually in danger. It is not a danger to you, nor is it a danger to me or to
other people."

It is also explained that feelings of contamination, often strong feelings, can be evoked by memories, thoughts, and pictures in the mind
(images)—without touching or even seeing a contaminant. Hence feelings of contamination can arise in surprising places or at surprising
times, such as sitting quietly alone at home.

6.7 Behavioral experiments

Behavioral experiments are mini-experiments that are carried out in
order to collect evidence which has a direct bearing on the patients' reasons for believing that they are under serious current threat. They are
particularly helpful because they provide the patient with direct, personal, vivid, and up-to-date information—which has greater value than
second- or third-hand information and greater evidential value than
random reading or random conversations. The evidence is fed into the
competing explanations, and not infrequently it tips the balance (notably, say, in treating a fear of morphing). Technically it is important for
the patient and therapist to formulate competing, unambiguous (written) predictions for each mini-experiment.

Some patients who have heard of, or received, exposure therapy mis-
takenly assume that the behavioral experiments are exposure exercises.
Unlike exposure exercises, which are deliberate, planned, repeated, prolonged exposures to the same situation or contaminated items
(called a "hierarchy of fear contaminants"), behavioral experiments are

circumscribed information-gathering exercises. There is no need to construct fear hierarchies in behavior experiments.

The experiments are not carried out repeatedly; once is generally sufficient. For example, Anil, who suffered from intrusive, objectionable, aggressive thoughts and impulses about harming his parents was convinced that if they learned what he was thinking about, they would reject and ostracize him. This expectation was set out in a written prediction and a behavioral experiment was undertaken to gather information about the effect of revealing to his parents his aggressive thoughts towards them. He learned from the experiment that his parents were kindly sympathetic about his problem and that they showed no fear of him. His apprehensive prediction was disconfirmed. There was no reason to repeat the experiment.

In the great majority of behavior experiments there is no reason to repeat or prolong the experiment. Although response prevention is an essential part of exposure treatment (ERP) it plays no part in behavior experiments.

If a patient is confused by the two techniques it is helpful to explain the different purposes of the two, and importantly to inform the patient that the specific mini-experiments are not prolonged and rarely repeated. The experiments are unlike exposure exercises in which it is expected and required that the patient repeatedly experiences significant levels of anxiety.

When patients undertake their behavioral experiments, if significant anxiety is experienced, as occasionally happens, it is regarded as a transitory discomfort that provides useful evidence, and it is rarely necessary to repeat the experiment. Response prevention plays no part in behavior experiments. See Table 6.1.

We recommend the following specific steps for the design of the behavioral experiment.

- Step 1—Consider the formulation. Collaboratively identify a key belief/thought/behavior/process that keeps the client stuck in the vicious cycle of perfectionism. Ask the client to rate how much he or she endorses that belief (0–100%)

Table 6.1 Comparison of behavioral experiments and exposure treatment.

	Behavioral experiment	**Exposure**
Primary purpose	To test the validity of a specific belief/s	To facilitate habituation—getting accustomed to the fear stimuli
Frequency	Usually once is sufficient	Exposures repeated many times
Systematically graded	No	Yes, generally from least frightening to most frightening; a fear hierarchy
Duration	Brief	Prolonged exposures, often for an hour or more
Anxiety	Not necessary to evoke anxiety	Essential to evoke anxiety
Response prevention	Irrelevant	Essential
Fear hierarchy	Not necessary to construct fear hierarchy	Fear hierarchy is constructed

- Step 2—Collaboratively decide on the form of an experiment to test the thought/belief/behavior/process. Ensure the experiment is not likely to be too challenging, and that it will likely yield useful and meaningful information. Be specific about when and where the experiment will be conducted.

- Step 3—Elicit specific predictions about the outcome of the experiment and devise a method to record the outcome (see record sheet in Appendix 9)

- Step 4—Anticipate problems and discuss possible solutions

- Step 5—Conduct the behavioral experiment

- Step 6—Review the experiment including the predictions, re-rate belief in the target belief, and draw conclusions

Activity 6.1: Your own experiment

Plan and conduct an experiment on one of your beliefs. Think about a behavioral experiment to test a belief you may hold about yourself, others, or the world. Beliefs about your standards, self-evaluation, pollution, washing, or other aspects relevant to mental contamination are particularly suitable.

6.8 **Imagery rescripting**

As mentioned, Beck (1976) observed that images often reveal important new information about the patient's disorder, and he used an elementary form of rescripting to overcome the images (pp. 152–157). Currently the most effective way of dealing with unwanted intrusive images is by tackling the image more directly, by changing the content and outcome of the image; by rescripting it. Most patients welcome the method and appreciate the control that it gives them over the unwanted images. The rescripting process is simple and straightforward and patients favor their preferred images. The technique is enhanced by discussing how the patient construes the original and then the preferred image (see Case 6.4).

A patient's maladaptive misinterpretation of the significance of the intrusive images can be tackled by the analysis of competing explanations of the meaning of the images, Explanation A vs. Explanation B.

In treatment, the occurrence, nature, frequency, and effects of the unwanted intrusive images are assessed, and rescripted as necessary. The patient and therapist establish the content of the disturbing intrusive images and then assess the effects of the selected image/s by using test probes (Hackmann et al., 2011).

A baseline is established by asking patients to form a clear, vivid image of a neutral scene, such as a country vista. Having ensured that they are not feeling contaminated, they are asked to form and hold the image for 1–2 minutes and then rate their feelings of contamination on a scale of 0–100 (where 0 = no contamination and 100 = intensely contaminated, the extreme of the continuum).

6.8.1 **Test probes**

The baseline level of contamination is checked again. Next they are asked to form a clear vivid image of the most disturbing of the selected scenes, hold it for 2–3 minutes, and then rerate their score on the contamination scale. If the first image fails to evoke a rating of at least 50%, the second most disturbing image is formed, and so on until a score in excess of 50% is evoked. The test probes are useful in assessment and in monitoring progress.

The important fact that feelings of contamination have been evoked without any physical contact with a contaminant is emphasized. As described in Chapter 1, contamination can be evoked by a disturbing image—or by a disturbing memory or disturbing thought, by a troubling conversation, or even by the sight of a feared/disliked person in the distance.

Patients are encouraged to use the rescripting in their everyday life and keep a record of how often they use the preferred image, and the frequency of the unwanted repugnant images. The records are discussed at the beginning of each therapy session. In most cases rescripting is readily and gladly generated. It provides relief and a welcome sense of control.

6.9 Relapse prevention

A relapse prevention plan is drawn up at the end of therapy. The plan includes a description of the factors that had maintained the client's contamination fear, the techniques the client had found useful in treatment, identifying potential triggers for setbacks, and considering ways of resolving future difficulties.

When the initial, general treatment of mental contamination has made progress the specific methods for dealing with the particular manifestations of the disorder are introduced. Detailed accounts of these techniques are given in Chapters 7–10.

Case illustrations of cognitive behavioral methods

Case 6.1 Explanation A vs. Explanation B

David was assailed by the fear that he might become contaminated by any of a range of items and places and anything at all related to his violator. During the assessment interview it emerged that the idea of being contaminated had various meanings for him, and his high responses to the Personal Significance Scale provided details of his appraisals. A major appraisal was that "my feelings of contamination mean that I am a weak and inadequate person."

In the usual manner the personal significance of his feelings/thoughts was used to construct two contrasting explanations, A vs. B. Explanation A, "I am weak and inadequate," was compared to Explanation B, "I have a psychological problem—fear of contamination—that is treatable and the problem is not evidence that I am a weak or inadequate person." The evidence for and against the two explanations was gathered and discussed in detail.

Before each session he filled in the PSS and, after a slow start in which there was little shift in his appraisals of significance, changes became evident prior to session 8. It then accelerated, and after ten sessions his major negative appraisal ("My feelings of contamination mean that I am a weak and inadequate person") had dropped to zero. The other negative items on the PSS showed corresponding declines. By the concluding session 12 his fear of contamination, avoidance, and compulsive behavior had declined to non-clinical levels.

Mohamed feared that if he was touched by an "undesirable" person or even came into the proximity of such a person, he would pick up that person's unacceptable qualities.

Explanation A: (i) if I come close to an undesirable person, or even see them very clearly, I will pick up their undesirable qualities, and (ii), if so, I need to wash intensively to protect myself.

Explanation B: (i) if I come close to or even see an undesirable person, I will *not* pick up any of their undesirable qualities. If this prediction is confirmed, then part (ii) of Explanation A will fall away—there will be no need to protect myself by compulsive washing.

Mohamed was able to compile a number of specific undesirable qualities that he might pick up (e.g., shouting and gesturing in public, developing a shabby appearance), and these expectations were tested in a few behavioral experiments. They were all disconfirmed.

Mohamed also feared that he might be seriously affected by "mind germs."

Explanation A was supported by the fact that many illnesses are caused by the infection of germs, and mental *illnesses* might also be contagious. Hence he avoided any contact with people who appeared to be mentally disturbed and, like similar patients with a fear of morphing, avoided walking in their "airstream." He avoided going anywhere near psychiatric wards or hospitals.

Explanation B, that mental illnesses are not contagious, was supported by the fact that nurses, psychologists, and doctors who care for mentally ill patients do not develop similar illnesses. It was ascertained that Mohamed had never heard of any person, friend, or relative who had developed a mental illness after visiting a psychiatric facility or hospital. He had never heard of anyone developing such an illness by proximity to a mentally disturbed person. A few behavioral experiments were conducted, including a visit to a psychiatric ward and deliberately walking in the airstream of a "weird" person. He accepted Explanation B and the fear of becoming contaminated steadily diminished and evaporated.

The method of contrasting explanations was used in the case of Tim who was housebound because of an intense fear of becoming contaminated by any and all items from the outside world. He believed that his fears were evoked by touching contaminated items and that it was essential to wash his hands intensively.

A second possibility was introduced in therapy: as a result of prolonged psychological violation he had developed mental contamination.

Two explanations were set out:

Explanation A: (i) my fear is always provoked by contact with specifiable, tangible dirty items, and (ii) the contamination is localized on my hands.

Explanation B: (i) my fear is easily evoked by a thought, memory, or image, and (ii) the contamination is not confined to my hands.

A few tests were carried out to assess the explanations. The first part of Explanation A, contact with dirty items evoking contamination, was confirmed. However, part (ii) was disconfirmed because memories and images of his violations also evoked contamination and it was widespread, not confined to his hands. He felt contaminated all over, inside and outside his body.

The support for both parts of Explanation B led to a shift in therapy away from ERP—repeatedly handling tangible dirty items—to a full analysis of his cognitions about the violations and the nature of his current threats. He responded well to a course of CBT.

Case 6.2 Conceptual re-orientation

Rozin and Fallon suggested that although disgust can be unmade by a process of "extinction by frequent exposure . . . conceptual reorientation might be a more effective method" (1987, p. 38). For example, disgust can be undone or reduced by cognitive reorientations, such as by informing the person that what he/she thought was rotten milk was actually yogurt, or that the forbidden pork was actually lamb after all.

Conceptual reorientation can act in the opposite direction and induce feelings of pollution.

Amy had developed feelings of disgust contamination that were evoked by any direct or indirect contact with her loathed former partner. On returning from work one evening she found a package outside her front door containing a take-out meal and a pair of woollen gloves. Believing that they had been left there by her ex-partner, she felt disgusted and knew that she could never eat the food or wear the gloves. She pushed the package aside and avoided handling the contents. She then telephoned her parents to tell them about this objectionable intrusion and was surprised to learn that the package had been left by her father. Instantly, the feelings of disgust disappeared and she ate the meal and tried on the gloves.

In one case, a patient's chronic, uncontrolled, intensive daily washing (including the use of bleach) was driven by her feelings of mental pollution. After completing a major reappraisal of her mistaken belief that she had behaved immorally, Shamsun was able to gain control of her compulsions. It emerged that she had in fact been manipulated by two members of her family who had misled her for their financial gain, and her sense of mental pollution and guilt were replaced by anger towards the relatives who had betrayed her. The reduction in her feelings of pollution/contamination was followed by a significant decline in her compulsive urges. Some supplementary sessions of ERP were sufficient to overcome years of uncontrollable washing.

Case 6.3 Survey

One of our patients, Elizabeth, felt contaminated when she was near her boyfriend's friends. Her boyfriend had been unfaithful a few years previously, and Elizabeth felt that his friends (who had known) had also betrayed her. She was guilty about avoiding her boyfriend's friends and it was causing problems between them. She felt it meant she was a bad person because she was unable to forgive her boyfriend's friends, even though she had been able to forgive her boyfriend. We constructed a survey asking people whom the patient regarded as upright and moral to answer the following questions:

Imagine your partner had been unfaithful a few years previously. A few of his friends knew about this infidelity.

1 How would you feel about the friends?

2 When you saw his friends, what would you be thinking?

3 Would you be able to forgive his friends for not telling you?

4 If you could not forgive his friends how would you feel about that?

As is the case with most surveys, there were a variety of responses. They ranged from "I would be angry with his friends" to "I don't blame the friends." Many felt they would be thinking about the infidelity when they saw the friends, and some felt they would be able to understand and forgive the friends but others felt they could not. There were lots of "depends" in the answers but very little guilt about whether they could/couldn't forgive them. The client learned that people have different reactions to such situations and she concluded that not being able to forgive her boyfriend's friends did not mean that she was a bad person.

Case 6.4 Imagery rescripting

In a straightforward example, a 45-year-old woman sought help for reducing her depression and stopping her recurrent, nasty, repugnant images of seriously harming her much-loved, ailing mother. After analysis, discussion, and some test probes, she opted for an image of approaching her mother with a happy smile and giving her a warm hug. She quickly learned to generate and enjoy the preferable image, and the recurrent repugnant image faded out within 3 weeks.

Ian (see Chapter 1) suffered from a nasty recurrent image of being humiliated and degraded by government officials who unjustly treated him as an irresponsible "deadbeat" father who was unwilling to provide support for his young son. After a full discussion and rehearsals of his preferred image, Ian chose to rescript the image into a friendly helpful scene. He succeeded in replacing the nasty upsetting intrusive images with benign rescripted images.

Case 6.5 Behavioral experiment

Caroline, aged 26, avoided contact with people whom she considered immoral. Her concerns had begun after her boyfriend was unfaithful and some of his friends had known about the betrayal. Her avoidance of immoral people had led her to be withdrawn socially and resulted in low mood. When she came into contact with immoral people she felt polluted and washed her hands and clothes excessively and drank lots of water to cleanse her body of perceived impurity. The behavioral experiment and record sheet shown in Table 6.2 was completed with Caroline.

Table 6.2 The behavioral experiment and record sheet as completed by Caroline

Situation	Predictions	Experiment	Outcome	What I learned
	What do I think will actually happen? How much do I believe it will happen (0–100%)? What will happen to my fear of contamination? How much do I believe this (0–100%)?	What can I do to test my fear of contamination? How can I find out what will happen to my fear?	What actually happened? Were any of my predictions correct?	What do I make of the experiment? How much do I believe my initial predictions will happen in future (0–100%)? How can I test this further?
Going to a sleazy part of town	I think I will get anxious and need to leave. I won't feel contaminated if I stay at home I believe this will happen (100%) I will feel completely contaminated and end up washing for hours (100%)	Perhaps go to a slightly sleazy part of town with a coat first of all and see what happens. I can compare this to what happens if I stay at home in terms of my contamination and washing	I did feel contaminated when I went to town with my friend and a coat, but I managed. I didn't leave. I saw a film and by the end it was OK. I did wash my clothes when I got home though. On the day I stayed home I felt isolated and pathetic because I was missing out, and actually felt dirty for some reason	I was surprised how quickly my feelings of dirtiness disappeared when I was watching the film and also how much worse it was staying in I revised my beliefs to 50% for feeling anxious and leaving the situation and for washing for hours I do need to test this though, by perhaps not wearing a coat, not going with a friend, going to a disreputable part of town. Maybe I won't wash my clothes in the end but that seems a way off at the moment.

Chapter 7

Contamination After Physical or Psychological Violations

Given that most instances of mental contamination are generated by being violated physically or emotionally, patients develop intensely negative feelings towards the violator. In therapy they are encouraged to adopt a defiant attitude, and behavior, because they have endured a double injustice. Not only have they been harmed and distressed by the violation but in addition they have been left with a dysfunctional psychological problem—a double injustice. The defiance flows from and is encouraged in therapy by a recognition of this double injustice.

For example, a young man felt polluted and engaged in compulsive cleaning whenever he received a (rare) telephone call from the perpetrator of his distress, the woman who had betrayed him. Another case of the development of feelings of pollution after a betrayal is described in Case 7.3 on page 123. Betrayals involve a loss of trust and are encountered in marriages, friendships, religious, financial, and work relationships (Rachman, 2010).

The affected person develops a fear/dislike of the people responsible for the violation, and the aversion is often accompanied by anger and avoidance. In addition to taking steps to avoid any direct or indirect contact with the violator, the affected person may engage in classical compulsive handwashing to remove the sense of contamination.

The intensity and degree of contamination fluctuate with changes in attitude and negativity towards the violator. If a reconciliation takes place, the contamination may even diminish. In one instance, after the violator sent an apology and a gift to the patient, the contamination set off by proximity to the clothing he had left behind in their flat declined from 100% contamination to 30%. The level and range of mental contamination fluctuate in concert with fluctuations in the patient's feelings and attitudes to the primary contaminator. If a breach recurs, the feelings of contamination return.

In many cases the patient is extremely angry with the perpetrator and repeatedly remembers and recounts particularly upsetting remarks or hurtful events. Hence, descriptions and discussions about people who have harmed the patient are included in the Contamination Standardized Interview Schedule provided in the Toolkit (Appendix 6). Information about the primary source of the mental contamination is essential in directing and facilitating treatment.

As discussed in Chapter 2, instances of violation greatly outnumber the incidence of significant mental contamination. At present we do not know what makes the difference—how do most people endure violations without developing significant feelings of pollution/contamination?

Possibly there is a pre-existing sensitivity to feelings of contamination among a minority of people, and for them the feelings are abnormally intense and persistent. Their resilience to contamination is inadequate. A major question is how and why the experience of violation comes to generate feelings of pollution and compulsive cleaning. One possibility is that the violator is regarded as an enemy and, as Rozin and Fallon (1987) observed, the person and possessions of an enemy evoke feelings of aversion and disgust. In a simple illustration, people avoid wearing or even touching the clothing of an enemy. Unavoidable contacts with a violator/enemy or his or her possessions readily generate feelings of pollution and compulsive washing.

7.1 Form of contamination after psychological violation

The diversity of psychological violations, ranging from betrayals to humiliations, painful criticisms, degradations, and beyond, requires a set of specific treatment techniques to deal with each manifestation. In helping patients whose fears of contamination are connected to these violations, clinicians use their broad knowledge and clinical experience, supplemented by the specific tactics.

Often the sense of violation emerges shortly after a period in which the perpetrator degraded, manipulated, betrayed, or humiliated the affected person. The violator/s and anything associated with them convey feelings of contamination which persist and inflate even in the absence of any physical contact.

In those instances where there is a large time gap between the violation and the emergence of the feelings of contamination/pollution the cause can be missed or overlooked. The connection between the violation and the feelings of contamination can be obscure and leave patients confused by their feelings of contamination. They sense a connection between the violation and their current feelings of contamination but are puzzled by the time gap: "Yes, but why *now*?" Answers to this question usually emerge during therapy. The delayed onset of feelings of pollution/contamination resembles the delayed onsets that occur in some cases of PTSD. During therapy attempts are made to understand the nature of the current threat.

A second source of perplexity arises from the difficulty which people, and perhaps patients in particular, experience when trying to describe or recognize the sense of internal dirtiness. Our concept of dirtiness entails physical contact with a tangible contaminating substance, but feelings of internal dirtiness lack the familiar characteristics of dirt. It looks clean but feels dirty. Lady Macbeth's attempts to clean her hands are a dramatic example of the confusion between internal pollution and external, localized dirt. In clinical circumstances, the fact that many patients with feelings of mental contamination also experience feelings of "ordinary" contamination can confuse diagnosis at the outset of assessment.

7.2 Treatment after physical violation

The guide for assessing and treating contamination fears that emerge after physical violation comes from the literature on PTSD (Ehlers and Clark, 2000). In that disorder, maladaptive cognitions include the appraisal that the trauma has caused irreparable damage to one's psychological stability, or personality, and/or to one's brain. The persistence of the PTSD symptoms of re-experiencing, hypervigilance, and disturbances of memory is interpreted as confirmation of permanent damage, and reinforces the patients' pessimistic expectations about their future. The intrusive symptoms and hypervigilance fuel a prevailing feeling of vulnerability and dread. As a result, the person's ability to cope is compromised.

In some cases of PTSD a fear of contamination is embedded in the disorder, particularly if the traumatic event/s involved sexual violation. Victims become hypervigilant to disturbing cues that are associated with the assault, and that includes feelings of mental pollution/contamination. The pollution is evocable by visual, olfactory, or verbal cues, memories, and images. The feelings are distressing and generate urges to decontaminate, to wash and clean. If the victim's PTSD symptoms are accompanied by feelings of unusual intangible dirtiness, mainly internal, hard to localize, or remove, easily evoked by memories or other mental events, then the presence of mental contamination is probable. This element of contamination is assessed in the usual manner by a combination of interviewing, tests of imagery, behavior tests and psychometrics, especially the scale for measuring mental contamination, VOCI-MC.

In PTSD resulting from sexual violation, the feelings and cognitions about mental contamination and disgust tend to predominate. The contamination is usually experienced as "internal dirtiness." Given the large number of victims of sexual assault who report signs of mental contamination, clinicians are alert to the possibility or even probability that their patients may be experiencing mental pollution/contamination. It is advisable routinely to assess victims of sexual assault for the presence of mental pollution/contamination and distressing internal dirtiness.

Three treatment goals are set out in the Ehlers and Clark guidelines: "Modify excessively negative appraisals of the trauma and its sequelae, reduce re-experiencing by elaboration of the trauma memories and discrimination of triggers, drop dysfunctional behaviours and cognitive strategies," (Ehlers et al., 2005, pp. 415–418). The treatment effects are large and stable and dropout rates are remarkably low. In a recent study of 330 patients with PTSD (age 17–83) who were treated in routine outpatient services, 85% of those who completed the treatment improved significantly (Ehlers et al., 2013).

The key cognitions pertaining to the fear of contamination are analysed and adaptive interpretations promoted. After progress on the cognitive side, a graded, gradual course of ERP can be directed at any tangible contaminants, if necessary. In the course of cognitive therapy for PTSD the patient may need to recall and sometimes even "re-experience" the traumatic events. These procedures are stressful, and as they occasionally revive or intensify the feelings of mental pollution/contamination, therapists take care to dampen any resurgences.

7.3 **Treatment after psychological violation**

The mechanism by which betrayals trigger intense feelings of contamination and mental pollution is not fully understood. There are elements of fear and disgust involved, but exactly why it takes the form of feelings of *contamination* rather than some other psychological problem, remains to be explained. As mentioned at the beginning of this chapter, it is possible that the violator is perceived as an enemy who arouses anger, aversion, and disgust; enemies often are regarded as sources of pollution. The aversion to possessions belonging to an enemy is so strong that people would rather freeze than wear clothes which belong to an enemy. They are a source of pollution.

A typical cognition is: "My feelings of distress and of self-abasement intensify with each reminder/contact with X (the primary source of the distressing events). It shows that I remain abnormally sensitive to the person and events involved and have been permanently harmed. I cannot cope and am at risk." This is similar to the unadaptive cognitions which develop in cases of PTSD—"these nasty, intrusive experiences are persisting and will never cease; I have been irreparably harmed and remain vulnerable." The repeated evocation of these distressing reactions in the presence of the primary or secondary sources of the contamination consolidates the appraisal that one is in danger of pollution and/or harm—*ex consequentia*. This is also supported by findings from the dirty kiss experiments described in Chapter 4, in which cognitions associated with betrayal, violation, and responsibility were highly predictive of contamination responses following listening to a recording of a non-consensual kiss (Elliott and Radomsky, 2013; Radomsky and Elliott, 2009).

Case illustrations of treatment of contamination after physical or psychological violations

Case 7.1 Treatment after physical violations

A schoolteacher, Jill, in her late 30s, felt compelled to wash her hands many times a day and take one to four hot showers per day. She also spent endless hours cleaning her kitchen and all of the carpets. Previous treatment, pharmacological and dynamic psychotherapy, had provided some relief, but the major problems were unchanged.

Her difficulties had developed 18 months earlier after an episode of depression that lasted for 16 weeks, during which she went on disability leave. When she was 8 years old she had suffered from several instances of sexual abuse, and after concealing the events for a while disclosed them to her parents, who took action that led to the perpetrator, a family friend, receiving a prison sentence. She was violated by the perpetrator, felt extremely angry towards him, and was resigned to believing that her life had been permanently damaged by the abuse.

Many years later the perpetrator was accused of committing more sexual assaults and the patient was asked to give evidence at the trial. Preparing a full account of the abuse, and having to discuss it with prosecutors, and finally giving evidence in open court was extremely upsetting and made her feel dirty and morally polluted. She became clinically depressed. The compulsive cleaning and prolonged hot showers emerged during the protracted legal proceedings.

Jill received 12 sessions of CBT, beginning with discussions of the nature and psychological effects of sexual abuse, including the mentally/morally polluting effects of abuse, and the availability of evidence-based treatments. Her cognitive appraisals were analysed and evaluated, and as progress was made she was encouraged to reduce and finally eliminate the compulsive handwashing. It was emphasized that the feelings of moral/mental pollution were not dirtying her hands, and hence washing them was misdirected. A similar rationale helped her to extinguish the daily hot showers.

At the end of therapy she was considerably improved. Her compulsive washing was down to near zero and the compulsive house cleaning ceased. She was more sociable and far less guarded. Additionally, her family was functioning more satisfactorily. Her children were once more free to invite friends over, and even bring their pets.

Case 7.2 Treatment after psychological violation

A man in his 40s sought treatment for OCD that had distressed him for many years. The main problem was compulsive handwashing in order to remove feelings of contamination. His mobility was severely restricted because of a pervasive fear of contamination. Almost all situations, inside or outside his home, were contaminated and each day he spent hours washing and cleaning. Early in treatment he was asked to bring four contaminated items to the clinic for "decontamination." One of them was a grungy outdated credit card that evoked a contamination score of 85/100. It had belonged to his stepfather who had died 8 years earlier—the contamination outlived him.

The patient's feelings of contamination developed at the age of 14 when his stepfather came to live in the family home. The patient resented the "intruder" who was incessantly critical of his appearance, speech, conduct, and character. The stepfather engineered his removal to an uncongenial boarding school, where he felt abandoned. The stepfather/violator was the focus of his feelings of contamination and everything associated with him was tainted. The patient's attempts to remove the contamination by compulsive handwashing were not successful, but he received some benefit from medications and behavior therapy.

The turning point in the course of CBT was his gradual recognition that the stepfather's rejection and prolonged degradation had left him feeling worthless and tainted—contaminated. Any direct or indirect contact with the stepfather, the human contaminant, was upsetting and polluting. The power of his late stepfather's outdated credit card to continue contaminating him for 8 years after the man's death speaks to the remarkably unchanging quality of many contaminants. After a full course of therapy, combining cognitive analyses and modification, plus three sessions of exposure exercises, which acted as a "fixing agent," he was much improved. The feelings of contamination and compulsive handwashing were substantially reduced, and his mobility was no longer restricted.

Case 7.3 Treatment after psychological violation involving betrayal

Amy developed mental contamination when she discovered that while she was away on a 3-day business trip her fiancé's former girlfriend had moved into the apartment with him. She was shocked and upset by his betrayal and demanded that he immediately leave her apartment with all his belongings and never contact her ever again. She felt disgusted and sullied by the contamination he left behind and had many hot showers. Her apartment was tainted and she gave it a thorough cleaning, using some disinfectants. She avoided all contact with her fiancé and his friends, and reported that even talking to him on the telephone made her feel contaminated. He had become a contaminant.

A few days after he left she was puzzled by the fact that many of her clothes looked and felt dirty. When they returned from the dry-cleaners they looked clean but still felt dirty to the touch, and she was unable to wear them. This is a common feature of mental contamination in which people, or objects, look clean but feel dirty, polluted. She developed intensive daily compulsive washing and showering.

The betrayal-induced mental contamination was treated by a combination of cognitive therapy and exposure exercises. The initial didactic sessions had an enlightening effect. In addition to the distress and discomfort she was experiencing, she was baffled and troubled by the nonsensical irrationality of feeling that her objectively clean clothes were dirty. It made no sense and fed her growing self-doubts.

It was explained that the victims of a betrayal often feel morally and physically polluted, and she was given information, including illustrations from case histories, to read. The occurrence of mental contamination was described, and she was impressed by the fact that the source of mental contamination is always human. She said that she certainly felt that her former fiancé had polluted her. The mere sight or sound of him evoked feelings of contamination, as did any object or place associated with him.

The injustice of a victim of betrayal struggling with persistent feelings of pollution was discussed and she decided actively to overcome them by defiance. These cognitive changes were then followed by a few sessions in which some exposures to contaminated items were undertaken. After a slow start she made significant progress and by the conclusion of the 12-session course the contamination had faded and she no longer washed compulsively.

Chapter 8

Self-Contamination

A less obvious but damaging form of mental contamination can arise from one's own thoughts/images/impulses. No physical contact with harmful substances is involved. In common with other forms of mental contamination, the primary source of the contamination is human not harmful substances. Paradoxically, in these cases the affected person is the source of his or her own contamination. Patients are tormented by recurring, uncontrollable repugnant thoughts/images/urges and subsequent feelings of contamination. Self-contamination can also arise from unacceptable actions, such as malicious acts, betrayal, harming others, and morbid preoccupation with pornographic material. Shame and guilt are the common accompaniments of self-contamination.

The concept of self-contamination seems absurd or, at least, paradoxical, but it does occur, however unknowingly. Clashes between repugnant intrusive urges/images and one's moral values can induce feelings of contamination, and intrusive, objectionable sexual thoughts, such as incestuous ones, are a particularly distressing source. Troubling dreams of an objectionable nature can also induce contamination. Memories can evoke contamination, just as the experimentally instructed formation of certain images can induce feelings of contamination (Coughtrey et al., 2014b; Fairbrother and Rachman, 2004; Fairbrother et al., 2005). The threat of recontamination is always present.

Intrusive, unacceptable sexual images and thoughts, such as molesting children or incest, are common sources of self-contamination. Moreover, the personal significance which the patient attaches to these thoughts and images is sometimes reinforced by dream fragments on these themes. Patients do not readily make a connection between their repugnant intrusive thoughts and the feelings of pollution and/or their compulsive cleaning.

Self-contamination can be provoked by personally unacceptable behavior, such as watching pornographic movies, masturbation, and internet pornography involving children. Bursts of cleaning often follow. In her study of unwanted, unwelcome thoughts in a subclinical OCD sample, Zucker (2004, p. 47) found that "sexual thoughts were significantly associated with cleaning compulsions." A particularly troublesome aspect of self-contamination is that the potential for triggering the contamination is always present. There are no time-outs.

In the religious domain, the experiences of Bunyan (1998) are a vivid example of the occurrence of mental pollution. He interpreted his stream of blasphemous thoughts as satanically sinful and was polluted by them. The mental events are unique to the person experiencing them. They can be described to other people, but the personal appraisals which the person makes of the significance of these mental events are unique. Lady Macbeth's thoughts about her terrible crime were unique and generated an overwhelming sense of pollution.

Objectionable sexual or aggressive dreams can be interpreted as confirmation of a suspected moral flaw. Given the connections between mood, depression, and obsessions (Ricciardi and McNally, 1995; Sutherland et al., 1983), it is probable that feelings of self-contamination vary with mood state, and that during periods of depression exacerbations of contamination are to be expected.

Feelings of contamination tend to be increased by criticisms, including self-criticism, but in most instances are unaffected by feelings of anger. These influences were illustrated by a patient whose bouts of washing increased significantly when she was criticized but were unchanged when she was angry.

The guilt and shame caused by emotionally and morally repugnant images, thoughts, impulses, and dreams is so distressing that they prevent patients from ever revealing their awful secrets. If and when patients overcome their prolonged concealment during therapy, it can be extremely emotional and leave the patient unburdened but upset. After the initial disclosure of the self-contaminating thoughts, further distressing revelations tend to follow. The overall therapeutic value of such disclosures needs to be determined, but in the short term they appear to give considerable relief and certainly help to focus the remaining sessions of therapy. When patients develop an improved, realistic interpretation of the significance of the self-contaminating thoughts, therapeutic progress follows. See Box 8.1.

Box 8.1 Beliefs and appraisals about self-contamination

- It is very important for me to be clean in body and in mind
- It is extremely difficult for me to block my unacceptable nasty thoughts
- Aggressive thoughts are always unworthy and unkind
- The best way for me to deal with unwanted and unacceptable sexual thoughts is to have a good wash
- It is wrong for me to have unwanted unacceptable thoughts or impulses
- An unwanted objectionable thought is as bad as an objectionable deed
- I feel tainted or dirty if I have a disgusting dream
- It is morally wrong for me to have thoughts of harming other people
- My unwanted unacceptable thoughts mean that there is something badly wrong with my character
- It is important for me to control my thoughts better
- I must always keep my mind clean and pure
- Unacceptable sexual thoughts or impulses make me feel dirty
- Having a good wash helps me to get rid of nasty unwanted thoughts
- Having unwanted unacceptable thoughts or impulses is a sign that I might lose control of myself one day
- If I have a really disgusting thought it makes me feel dirty and tainted

> **Box 8.1 Beliefs and appraisals about self-contamination** *(continued)*
>
> - It is important for me to conceal my repugnant thoughts
> - Having unwanted unacceptable thoughts or impulses means that I might lose control of myself one day
> - If I have a truly disgusting thought it makes me feel tainted
> - I must try harder to control my thoughts
> - I must never ever have disgusting thoughts or impulses
> - Having repugnant thoughts makes me feel like a bad, wicked person

Personalized beliefs and appraisals drawn from this list can be helpful during assessment and treatment. Tracking patients' interpretations of their uninvited thoughts by administering the PSS at the beginning of each session is used to assess the progress of therapy. The scores indicate which interpretations are changing; those which are not changing require extra attention.

8.1 **Treatment of self-contamination**

In many cases of self-contamination the feelings of contamination and pollution are stirred up by intrusive and objectionable thoughts, images, and urges. If a patient suffering from obsessions shows signs of avoiding contaminants, the presence of mental contamination is assessed by a combination of special interviewing, psychometrics, imagery, and behavior tests. If the feelings of contamination are being provoked and/or sustained by obsessions then a course of cognitive treatment for the intrusions should be considered. In these cases, as in other instances of mental contamination, some manifestations of contact contamination are evident and need to be tackled.

The cognitive-behavioral treatment of obsessions provides a bridge for the treatment of self-contamination that is driven by distressing intrusions. The technique for treating obsessions is derived from the cognitive theory that obsessions are caused by a catastrophic misinterpretation of the personal significance of one's unwanted intrusive thoughts (Rachman, 2003; Whittal et al., 2010; see also Clark and Beck, 2011; Clark and Purdon, 1993; Freeston et al., 1997). The aim of the treatment is to help patients replace the maladaptive interpretations of their thoughts with more appropriate and adaptive construals. To the extent that the patient succeeds in this task, the duration and frequency of the obsessions diminish and even disappear. Once accomplished this paves the way to reducing or eliminating the self-contamination.

The clinical observations are consistent with the statistical association between obsessions and contamination. Scores on the Obsessions subscale of the VOCI correlate 0.57 with scores on the VOCI-MC scale among people diagnosed with OCD (Radomsky et al., 2014). Repugnant thoughts, images, and impulses are highly significant for an understanding of mental contamination in general and self-contamination in particular. It also highlights the importance of a thorough assessment of unwanted thoughts, images, and impulses in association with contamination-related problems, as well as the development of a case conceptualization that incorporates both obsessions and mental-contamination phenomenology (see Shafran and Radomsky, 2013).

Patients are given important information about the nature of mental contamination and feelings of self-contamination. This provides great relief because they are burdened by a secret fear and feel that they are weird. This sensitive information is discussed with considerable care, and it paves the way for treatment. A full copy of the information that can be provided for patients is contained in the Toolkit (Appendix 9).

Certain obsessions are prone to induce feelings of self-contamination. Repugnant sexual obsessions, such as molesting a child and incestuous images, are prime examples. If the images, or dreams, are misinterpreted as expressions of objectionable intentions, the person may think that the obsessions reveal a lurking, repulsive part of his or her true character, and feel polluted. The feelings of internal dirtiness and pollution instigate attempts at physical and/or mental cleansing.

Obsessions in which the person fears that he/she might attack or harm someone, known or unknown, can also generate feelings of self-contamination. These intrusive feelings can become uncontrollable and exceedingly distressing. As the source of the contamination, one's self, is always present, the threat of recontamination is constant. There is no period of safety.

When the self-contamination is linked to obsessions, the treatment is an amalgam of CBT for obsessions and for contamination. The patient's cognitions pertaining to the obsessions and to the feelings of contamination are analysed and a compilation is made of the evidence for and against the person's interpretations. The planning of treatment, and the assessment of progress, is facilitated by the use of the Scale for measuring the personal significance which the patient places on the main obsessions (PSS—see Appendix 5). The patient completes the PSS at the start of each session. When necessary, and it often is necessary, behavior experiments are constructed in order to collect direct, personal evidence (Rachman, 2003).

As progress is made in unravelling the patient's unadaptive/erroneous interpretations of the significance of the obsessions and contamination fears, behavioral experiments, and ERP, can be used if any contact contamination lingers after the cognitive progress.

Case illustrations of the treatment of self-contamination

Case 8.1

The treatment of Ben who engaged in heavy washing every day, occasionally several times per day, is an instructive illustration of the effectiveness of a behavior experiment. He was a member of a close and affectionate family and went to the family home each weekend to join in the congenial Sunday lunches, but he was plagued by repeated images of attacking members of the family. The images were so vivid and intense that he avoided going into the family kitchen lest he snatch a knife and stab someone.

The images made him feel so polluted and disgusted that Ben took lengthy hot showers—but to no avail. He had given up his many attempts to block or suppress the horrifying images because they were ineffective. The patient was filled with self-doubt, defeated by the problem, and gloomy about his future.

Following the didactic sessions, work began on modifying the significance that Ben attached to his frightening and hateful images. Steady progress was made, and a behavior experiment had a major impact. His family knew that he was depressed and receiving treatment but were unaware of the nature of the problem. He was understandably reluctant to disclose to his parents the content of his terrible images and was certain that they would react very badly and ostracize him.

By gradual steps he reached the point when he felt he would be able to disclose to them the nature of his dreadful and embarrassing problem, and a behavior experiment was undertaken. After two rehearsals Ben succeeded in telling them what ailed him. To his happy surprise they were kind and understanding and asked how they could help him.

The following weekend Ben went to his parents as usual. He was asked to describe in detail what happened:

His mother opened the front door

THERAPIST: Did she appear to be frightened of you?

PATIENT: *No, of course not*

THERAPIST: Did she refuse to let you enter?

PATIENT: *No*

THERAPIST: Did she threaten to call the police?

PATIENT: *Of course not*

THERAPIST: Did she give you her usual hug?

PATIENT: *Yes*

THERAPIST: All this despite the fact that you had told them you had repeated images of attacking and harming them?

PATIENT: *Yes. Kind of hard to believe*

THERAPIST: It seems as if they didn't interpret your images in the same way that you do

PATIENT: *I guess so*

THERAPIST: They didn't change their behavior to you, and didn't react as if you are a dangerous person. Not dangerous

PATIENT: *That's right*

THERAPIST: Needs thinking about

PATIENT: *Yes, I agree*

The significance of the behavior experiment was discussed in subsequent sessions and had a considerable impact on the patient's interpretation of the meaning of his images. As his PSS scores declined, the frequency and intensity of the images faded out and his compulsive cleaning ceased. He remained well at follow-up.

Case 8.2

A young man was extremely disturbed by intrusive thoughts that, against his wishes, he might sexually molest a child. He therefore took great care to avoid being alone with children or even walking past places where children congregate. He believed that he was a latent pedophile. When he encountered children he was tormented by doubts about whether he had looked at them inappropriately, and whether he had touched them or spoken to them inappropriately.

As a result he was tensely vigilant in their presence and confused and troubled by his bodily sensations. He was unsure whether his sweaty hands and thumping heart meant that he was sexually aroused or anxious. These confusing sensations set off the frightening possibility that one day he might lose control and actually molest a child. His belief that he was a pedophile led him to avoid long-term relationships because he had decided that under no circumstances would he risk having children of his own. His emotional and sexual relationships were in other respects satisfactory.

The occurrence of the intrusive and repugnant thoughts on the subject of pedophilia made him feel dirty, untrustworthy, and distressed. He tried to block or suppress the intrusions but found that this merely increased their frequency. Washing his hands vigorously provided short-term relief, but at times he felt obliged to shower repeatedly (e.g., after a disturbing dream in which children featured). At its worst he was washing 10–20 times per day and having repeat showers three or four times per week.

He described how at the age of 8–9, he had been sexually abused for approximately 18 months by the father of his friend, and when he defied the abuser by disclosing what was taking place, the perpetrator was prosecuted.

The patient gradually provided details of these events during therapy and by session 6 related that the abuser had said to him on several occasions that, "We are alike, we both enjoy these games, and when you grow up, you will be like me and enjoy playing our games with children. We are the same." The patient believed this assertion, and only started to search for information about pedophilia at the age of 13 after he saw a television program in which the topic was mentioned. In his secret untutored search he found references to the "cycle of abuse" and these confirmed his fear that he was a pedophiliac and trapped in an inescapable cycle.

After completion of the didactic phase of treatment, in which the nature and frequency of unwanted intrusive thoughts were explained, an analysis of his confusing reactions to children was carried out. A comparison was made between his fear of heights and his feelings and reactions in the presence of children, and they appeared to be similar—sweaty hands, racing heart, uneasiness. However, a description of his feelings during sexual events with his partner was different—positive desire and anticipation, nil avoidance, increased heart rate, nil sweaty palms, satisfaction, and no fear.

Some behavior experiments were carried out in order to collect direct personal evidence pertaining to the analysis, and also to compare the time course of his sexual feelings with his partner and the time course of his reactions to heights and to children. The uneasy anticipation and bodily reactions to walking across a city bridge were charted, with particular interest in the onset and offset of the unpleasant bodily sensations. The sensations and uneasiness were evoked well before reaching the bridge, and ceased when the walk was completed.

The time course of his feelings towards his sexual partner was different, with a gradual build-up that intensified to a climax, followed by a slow fading of pleasure. In the hours before the event he had thoughts about the anticipated intimacy but few bodily sensations; these were evoked in the sexual situation itself. Additionally, the feelings in the sexual event were completely different from the fear that he experienced on trips to the bridge, and different to his feelings when he saw children. The patient was enabled to discriminate efficiently between his thoughts/reactions in the sexual and the other circumstances. After completing the cognitive analysis and the behavior experiments he no longer felt confused about the meaning of his thoughts and bodily sensations in the presence of children. He concluded that it was fear arousal not sexual arousal.

The deep belief that he was a potential pedophile, a belief insinuated by the abuser, was approached by tackling the concept of a cycle of abuse. The patient was encouraged to carry out research into the revelations about the sexual abuses perpetrated by some priests in the Boston area. He learned that many of the people who had helped to expose the abuses—and worked for justice for the victims and to terminate the scandals—were themselves victims of childhood sexual abuse. In these instances, and in many other similar circumstances, so far from being drawn into an inescapable cycle of abuse, the victims actively opposed such abuse and successfully ended it.

The information changed his views about the nature and consequences of child-hood sexual abuse and he no longer felt destined to develop into a child molester. For a short period he continued to have occasional unwanted intrusive thoughts about children but was able easily to dismiss them. His cognitions and beliefs were substantially modified and newly adaptive, and the obsessions and mental contamination faded away. His thoughts no longer made him feel dirty and the compulsive washing came to an end.

Case 8.3

A woman in her early 20s sought help in struggling against her compulsive handwashing. Whenever she experienced strong feelings of dirt-contamination she felt driven to wash repeatedly, taking up to 60 minutes per day. She found it difficult to give a clear description of the contamination but was able to confirm that it was a type of uncomfortable, internal dirtiness and was definitely under her skin. In some ways it resembled ordinary feelings of dirtiness but was invisible and all over her body. The contamination was spontaneously evoked by thoughts, images, or memories but was also generated by physical contact with certain objects or with her bodily products.

The onset of the compulsions was traced to a period during which she had been distressed by intrusive, repugnant incestuous images. She was deeply ashamed, guilty, polluted, and distressed by the images and concealed them for years prior to starting treatment. She strongly resisted the images, but without success, and her self-esteem was damaged by the obsessions. The images were interpreted as a sign of some latent and disgusting element in her character, and as she was incapable of controlling the images, she feared that some day she might lose control of her behavior. By trial and error she had found that some transient relief was attainable by repeatedly washing her hands, but the abhorrent images and their damaging effects on her self-appraisal persisted until she received treatment.

In this case of self-contamination the feelings of pollution were a combination of internal dirtiness and moral repugnance, evocable by mental events, and with minimal contact with a visible contaminant. The feelings of dirt-contamination were not properly responsive to her repeated cleaning. During treatment she learnt how to construe and deal with the intrusive images and thoughts, and as their frequency and intensity declined, her fears and compulsive washing diminished significantly.

Case 8.4

Another patient obtained temporary relief from anxiety by compulsive washing after he experienced unwanted, repugnant thoughts of a sexual and aggressive nature that left him feeling polluted and "mentally dirty." He also used repeated hot showers to reduce his general sense of mental pollution. "Whenever I feel that I am a bad, dirty person, having a good shower makes me feel a bit better." The obsessions were greatly reduced during CBT, and the compulsive washing faded.

Case 8.5

A 22-year-old salesman complained of agitated depression that was harming his relationships, family attachments, and occupation. He was distressed and nearly disabled. It emerged that he was repeatedly experiencing vivid images of having sex with his 15-year-old sister. He was shocked and shamed by the images, which left him feeling morally and physically polluted. His strenuous attempts to block and suppress the images were unsuccessful, and taking lengthy hot showers gave him slight but transient relief. During and after the showers his body was clean, but he continued to feel internally dirty.

Following two didactic sessions in which he learned about the ubiquity of unwanted intrusive thoughts and how they can turn into uncontrollable obsessions if their meaning is badly misinterpreted, attention was focused on the significance which he attached to the recurrent images. Progress was made and he was advised to inhibit his unsuccessful attempts at blocking and suppressing. Initially he felt guilty about giving up his attempts to inhibit the images, but gradually succeeded. Similarly he took a while to inhibit his urges to take hot showers and to wash excessively, but eventually succeeded.

His changed interpretation of the significance of the images, confirmed by his weekly scores on the PSS, was accompanied by a substantial decline in his anxiety and depression. After 12 sessions he was significantly improved and remained well at the 6-month follow-up.

In cases where part of the problem is repugnant sexual cognitions that induce feelings of contamination, the affected person may confuse bodily sensations of anxiety (e.g., pounding heart, sweating, flushing) with those of sexual arousal. As Case 8.2, when a person who is tormented by fears of pedophilia comes near to children, he/she may misinterpret the bodily sensations of anxiety as a sign that he/she is responding sexually. These disturbing misinterpretations are best treated by the provision of corrective information, cognitive analysis, and behavior experiments.

Case 8.6

A patient who was receiving treatment for his pedophiliac obsessions had occasional dreams in which children featured, and interpreted them as confirming that he had sexual urges towards children. The disturbing dreams polluted him and he took hot showers for relief, but with little effect. In this, as in similar cases, the problem is not an interpretation of dreams but a *mis*interpretation of dreams. The patient benefitted from a 12-session course of CBT and was symptom-free at the conclusion.

Case 8.7

The problems of an introverted 21-year-old student were complex. In addition to her aggressive and sexual obsessions, she experienced episodes of panic, had an impoverished social life, and was moderately depressed. As the distressing obsessions occurred every day and were her primary problem, they were selected as the focus of treatment.

Her sexual obsessions consisted of inappropriate images, and impulses to make explicit suggestions to members of her family, friends and, occasionally, strangers. The thoughts and impulses, which involved rough and crude language, were completely alien to her. A proportion of the sexual obsessions were also aggressive. She avoided a variety of situations and people and engaged in strenuous and protracted washing for 1–4 hours per day. Her hands and arms, up to the elbows, were abraided and sore. The urges to wash were provoked by her "bad thoughts" which horrified her. She felt ashamed, guilty, and polluted. Sexual/aggressive dreams upset her and she was obliged to have an extended hot shower to rid herself of the dirtiness before starting her day. The compulsive washing gave some temporary relief but did nothing to ease her shame and self-denigration. Test probes, in which she formed some of her obsessional images, consistently produced feelings of pollution and an urge to wash.

After a course of CBT that was directed at her obsessions and feelings of self-contamination, she progressively reinterpreted her obsessions as non-significant intrusive thoughts. The self-denigration and interpretation of the obsessions as revealing that she was wicked and that she had a permanent flaw in her character gradually evaporated, and the compulsive washing then declined into non-significance. No ERP exercises were required. Construing the problem as one of self-contamination and treating it accordingly was successful. Despite these useful gains, her social life did not improve appreciably and she had patches of low mood that lasted for a few days at a time.

Case 8.8

Some cases of self-contamination arise out of actions. A middle-aged man from a highly religious background sought treatment for his prolonged compulsive washing and associated depression. It turned out that the main trigger for his washing was the frequent use of pornographic material, which left him feeling degraded and polluted. Thoughts about the material also produced feelings of pollution, but they were less intense and did not always trigger the washing.

The treatment consisted of a combination of cognitive therapy that focused on his inflated interpretation of the significance of his interest in pornographic material, and how he interpreted his sense of pollution (as a major, deep-seated, and permanent flaw in his character that darkened his whole life). As he made progress in reappraising the significance of his interest in pornography, he was encouraged to reduce the frequency and duration of his compulsive washing. He managed to do so, and his depression diminished.

Chapter 9

Morphing

A remarkable type of contamination arises from a fear that one might be tainted or changed by proximity to "disreputable" people or classes of "disreputable" people. The undesirables are unusual in their appearance or behavior and generally living on the fringes of the community. They are regarded as weird, immoral, mentally unstable, dirty, of low status, or a mixture of these characteristics. The fear can be provoked with or without physical contact, and affected patients strictly avoid these people.

In extreme instances the fear can go beyond a dread of being tainted or changed by the characteristics of the "undesirable" person. The affected person fears that his or her personality might be transformed by the undesirable person (*morphed*). "I fear that if I continue to look at him I might morph into him," "I will become like him," "I will become as weird as him," "If he repeatedly approaches me I will become as useless, ineffective, and incapable as him."

The mere sight of the person or persons is aversive and can raise the threat of being altered by their undesirable characteristics, by *visual contamination*. "If I keep looking at him then I might become like him or turn into him; I must avoid staring." In most cases the aversive reaction to the "undesirable person" includes an element of distaste or even disgust. It is embarrassing to admit that one is put off or disgusted by other people or classes of people, and sufferers from a fear of morphing tend to be ashamed of their feelings and attempt to conceal them. Expressing an aversion to classes of people is regarded as unjust and prejudicial, and hence shameful.

The fear of being contaminated by undesirable/weird people increases with the duration of the exposure, and the affected person is paradoxically drawn to stare at the threat. The fear can also be provoked, less commonly, by "auditory contamination," such as an unwanted telephone call from an undesirable or immoral person.

The fearful thoughts about morphing can be intrusive and disruptive and impair the person's ability to concentrate. At their worst these unwelcome intrusions displace the patients' other thoughts and interfere with their work and social behavior. Attempts to block or suppress the thoughts rarely succeed in overcoming the problem. After a close encounter, powerful urges to wash or neutralize dominate any competing behavior.

In a calm state the patients recognize the irrationality of the fear that they will somehow be morphed, and resist the idea. They are not delusional and function tolerably well at work and socially, while struggling to cope with their psychological problem. The link between a fear of morphing and a fear of contamination is evident from the fact that most of the patients who report fears of morphing also have typical fears of contamination, past or present. For example, a patient who feared that if he stared at weird people, their weirdness would be transferred to him, also suffered from a fear of being contaminated by harmful chemicals.

The belief is that proximity or visual or physical contact with disliked/despised persons *will change me* in particular. I will be unwillingly changed for the worse and may even morph into one of them. "If I come close to or merely see a weird person or someone who is evidently mentally ill, against my will I might be damagingly changed by them and come to resemble them." In some cases the patients try to make sense of their fears by drawing an analogy with the transmission of infections. Just as flu is contracted by proximity to an infected person—the virus is airborne—so they feel that "mind germs" might be airborne and transmit mental instability or mental illness. They avoid coming close to obviously unstable people because they believe that mental illnesses are contagious. If they do come too close, it commonly triggers compulsive decontaminating cleaning or mental cleansing. "Most illnesses are contracted by contact with infected people or substances that carry germs. People who are suffering from a mental *illness* carry germs—*mind germs*." These germs can be transferred by direct or indirect contact.

The contamination is acquired by a process of mental assimilation with little or no physical contact, and the feelings of contamination can be perceived as a threat to one's mental stability. Some patients ascribe the contamination to the effects of contagious mind germs. The underlying fear is that they are susceptible to a perplexing form of contamination, in which strange germs can transmit their harmful effects remotely and cause mental damage. The threat of mental contamination by germs is reinforced by the fact that when they do come into physical contact with an undesirable/weird person they experience feelings of contamination and need to wash themselves. Moreover, they feel that after a thorough wash they have removed the mind germs.

Fears of contracting mental instability or mental illness by contagion are uncommon but can reach clinically significant levels. It is possible that a *mild* belief in the possible contagiousness of mental illness is more common than is recognized, and somewhat similar beliefs prevail in diverse cultures.

For people who are seriously affected, the fear of morphing is a source of embarrassment because they know that the belief is regarded as absurd and expressing it can lead to ridicule. The fear can be manifested openly or indirectly. Less obvious manifestations are the seemingly inexplicable avoidances, such as people who travel long distances to avoid coming within sight of mental hospitals, or who avoid touching anyone associated with mental illness, or who avoid all mention of mental illnesses. A highly motivated competent trainee nurse who had a fear of morphing changed his career when he was informed that his next clinical rotation would involve working for 2 days per week in a psychiatric clinic.

Other terms that are used to explain the threat of a mental contagion are "goof germs" and "thought germs." Given this belief, affected people keep away from psychiatric hospitals or wards and strenuously avoid people who are known to be mentally ill and people who appear to be behaving strangely (e.g., shouting to themselves and gesturing in public). It should be emphasized that people who are troubled by a fear of morphing are neither ignorant nor delusional, and most of them function reasonably well despite their fears.

The strange and unusual quality of the fear of morphing is itself a source of extra anxiety and can fuel deeper fears of adverse changes in personality or losing one's mental stability. Therapists therefore provide corrective information about the nature and occurrence of the fear of morphing, and reassurance that there is no evidence that it is a way station towards a mental illness. Nurses, doctors, and psychologists who care for patients with mental illness do not pick up their illness. It is not contagious. Morphing patients are able to function moderately well despite the fear.

In order to bring some balance to the patients' fear that proximity to undesirable people might taint and damage their personality, it can be most helpful collaboratively to construct a list of the patient's most valued characteristics and traits and emphasize those which the patient is confident will never change.

With the exception of fictional accounts such as Kafka's masterpiece *The Metamorphosis*, in which Gregor Samsa awakens to find himself transformed into a gigantic insect (Kafka, 1983 edition), the psychological fear of morphing is confined to a fear of being adversely affected by undesirable characteristics of other *people*. See Box 9.1.

Box 9.1 Beliefs and appraisals about a fear of morphing

- It is best to avoid staring at people who look weird
- I am too easily influenced by some people who behave badly
- Quite a few people think that I am weak-minded and ineffective
- My own identity might be affected if I spend too much time with mentally unstable people
- It is best to wash very carefully if you touch the possessions or clothing of a weird person
- It is easy to pick up germs from mentally unstable people
- I often think that I have a weak personality
- It is best to avoid coming close to people who look mentally unstable
- My own identity might be affected if I spend too much time with weird people

Box 9.1 Beliefs and appraisals about a fear of morphing *(continued)*

- I worry that someday I will have a breakdown and be completely unable to cope
- It is best to avoid touching a person who seems to be mentally unstable
- Coming close to someone who looks weird makes me feel unclean even if I don't actually touch the person
- It is best to avoid staring at people who appear to be mentally unstable
- Some forms of mental instability are contagious and can be picked up by contact
- I am very easily influenced by other people
- It is best to avoid touching a weird person
- Staring at a nearby person who appears to be mentally unstable can make me feel unclean
- Weird people can influence me without my knowledge
- It is best to avoid coming close to people who look weird
- At times I worry that my fears about weird, shabby people might give me a breakdown
- It is best to wash very thoroughly if you touch the possessions or clothing of a mentally unstable person
- Sometimes I fear that I might lose my identity

9.1 **Treatment of morphing**

The fear of morphing involves unusual and idiosyncratic beliefs. Affected people assume that they can pick up undesirable characteristics from proximity to weird/abnormal/freakish people. The "undesirable" characteristics—mental instability, immorality, mental deterioration, drug addiction, weak character, freakish appearance or behavior— are believed to be transmissible by contact with people who manifest these characteristics, or by close proximity to them. It can develop by non-physical contact and commonly by visual contamination at a distance. It can also be caused or exacerbated by receiving disturbing negative information about a person or group of people.

The beliefs are amenable to change by the provision of corrective information and cognitive modification, along the following lines. The affected people recognize the irrational quality of the fear and in most other ways function satisfactorily. When fresh authoritative information is provided the beliefs tend to weaken but persist. The didactic component can be powerful. Behavioral experiments can have a significant impact on treatment and are easy to construct and carry out.

The treatment of morphing involves the general cognitive techniques, followed by those specific to morphing. The maladaptive cognitions about the perceived threat to one's personality, and about the (human) sources of contamination, are the basis of the disorder. The evidence supporting or negating the maladaptive cognitions is evaluated, and behavior experiments and surveys are carried out to collect fresh, personal information pertaining to the validity of the cognitions.

In the course of treatment patients are encouraged to compile a list of their desirable and approved characteristics and beliefs which are so well-grounded and stable that they are most unlikely to undergo any significant change. This information about their well-grounded, stable characteristics—"safe" aspects of their personality such as kindness, intelligence, empathy, friendliness—is then incorporated into the analyses of Explanation A vs. Explanation B.

Rescripting of disturbing images of oneself and/or of feared changes in behavior can be extremely effective. If the person has notably low self-esteem it is advisable to include self-appraisal in the cognitive analysis and modification. Avoidance behavior is discouraged. Treatment tends to progress smoothly in a logical fashion.

During the assessment it is necessary to determine whether the patients' fear of an invasion of their personality is a manifestation of OCD or a symptom of a psychotic illness. In cases of OCD, (i) the fear of morphing is recognized by the affected persons to be irrational, (ii) they recognize that the anxious thoughts/images about morphing are the product of their own mind and not alien intrusions controlled by some malicious outside source or outside force, (iii) they are well-functioning in most aspects of their life (occupationally, socially, personally), and (iv) they have no history of any psychotic illness.

Occasional patients raise the problem of the transmission of certain diseases, such as syphilis, which if left untreated can eventually damage the CNS and cause mental deterioration. This potential source of confusion can be dealt with by explaining the cause of the disease, by sexual contact, its treatability, its rarity nowadays, and the impossibility of contracting the disease by incidental proximity.

In the course of therapy, the didactic component is used to generate behavior experiments in order to help the patient collect personally significant corrective information. Questions that can help to plan behavior experiments include the following examples: "Has it ever happened to a relative of yours, or a friend of yours? Has it ever happened to you? If a friend or relative of yours walks close to or touches a disturbed person do they pick up any strange or weird behavior?"

On the basis of the cognitive analysis and the experiments, the behavioral component of therapy is introduced. The patient is encouraged to engage in planned exposures to the threat figures and places. The tactic of response prevention (inhibiting the washing, neutralizing, mental cleansing) is incorporated into the plan.

Some affected people attempt to protect themselves from morphing by "mental cleansing," and this tactic in also resorted to in other cases of mental contamination, especially self-contamination, and mental pollution. Patients are advised to refrain from such cleansing, to inhibit their urges to avoid people and places in which they anticipate worrying about morphing, and to refrain from any compulsive cleaning away of the effects of a visual contamination.

Adjusting the program of exposures as required, the anxiety, avoidance, and neutralizing decline progressively. The strongest fear of morphing is evoked by physical contact with the "undesirable" person, and hence a reduction of this part of the fear also weakens the effects of non-physical contacts. As fears generally collapse downwards from most frightening to least frightening, the therapist attempts to deal with the strong fears as soon as some progress has been made and the patient's motivation and expectations are judged to be sufficiently high. In treating cases of contamination it is necessary for the therapist, and patient, to titrate the exposure. It often becomes a matter of making speed slowly.

Cognitions selected from the list of common beliefs and appraisals in cases of morphing, set out in Box 9.1, are "personalized" for use in the assessment and cognitive analysis stages of the treatment. The therapist pays particular attention to the patient's belief, whether expressed directly or implied, that people can be morphed or transformed. Careful and repeated conversations about the belief and its basis are advisable.

It is helpful to compile a list of *desirable and approved beliefs and characteristics* which are so well grounded and stable that they are most unlikely to ever change.

Case illustrations of the treatment of morphing

Case 9.1

This transcript comes from the treatment of an accountant in her late 30s suffering from a fear of pesticides/diseases, compulsive washing and checking, religious obsessions, and a fear of morphing. In addition to the OCD, she suffered from low self-esteem, anxiety, and chronic pessimism. This extract concentrates on the features of morphing, the provision of information about the disorder, and the collection of evidence about the nature of the patient's perceived threats.

Her OCD started at the age of 15 during a period of family stress in which she was repeatedly criticized and denigrated by her parents, and it persisted into adulthood. She experienced unpleasant feelings of contamination and threat whenever she encountered "unfortunate" people who looked weird or disturbed and/or shabby and dirty. The feelings were evoked by the sight of such people, by visual contamination, or by physical proximity, and were especially intense if she touched them or their possessions. She avoided such people and the places where she was likely to encounter them. The feelings evoked by contacts were intrusive and unpleasant, and she dealt with them by vigorous washing.

When you see them how does that make you feel?

Fifteen feet away I'm comfortable, but 5 feet away I avoid them and even avoid their airspace

What happens if you can't avoid or it is too late to avoid them?

It is usually outside, so there is nowhere to wash. I feel the need to touch an unrelated object or recite a safe phrase under my breath until I can have a good wash

If you are near a washroom what do you do?

Well, if I have physical contact it would depend. If the person touched my hands I would have to wash them, and if she touched my clothing I'd have to wash it

What are you thinking of when you wash?

I'm getting a sense of relief. Uhmm, from any real or imagined germs . . . . And I know that it will trouble me until I do wash. Can't get it out of my mind. Here is an example: an odd-looking man dropped his parcel, a sort of blanket affair, as he tried to climb onto the bus and I picked up his stuff and helped him get on. I had to wash my hands before I could do anything else. I was like catatonic. I absolutely had to wash before doing anything else. One good long wash

What were you thinking? Were you protecting yourself?

Yes

From what?

From what? Misfortune

So that is why you avoid them?

Because I get frightened if they come near me

What happens if you fail to avoid them?

I get upset and rush to the nearest washroom to clean myself

Does that help you?

Usually, but it can take quite an effort

Why does washing give you some relief?

Because I am cleaning away the germs

Are these ordinary germs?

No, they are thought germs

The kind that you can pick up without any form of contact?

Yes, even from walking in a person's airspace

What do you think is the evidence for these germs?

Touching these people gives me the same feeling I get from touching say a dirty bandage

The feeling is the same?

Yes

Any other evidence you can think of?

It's not really evidence, but mental illness is an illness

I see. Is there any reason to expect that it is a contagious illness?

I don't see why not

Do people who work with mentally ill patients pick up the mental illness?

Not that I am aware of

Anyone at all?

No

How much do you know about mental illness?

Not a lot

Do you know anyone who is mentally unstable? Or ever hear about an acquaintance or friend who turned mentally unstable?

No

Have you ever read about someone turning mentally unstable after walking into contaminated airspace? The sort that worries you?

No, I haven't

If you encounter a person who is well dressed and clean, no germs, but behaving strangely, say talking aloud and making weird gestures, what would your reaction be if he came close or touched you?

I would have to wash. He is having some problem. Well, I might become like them, mentally unstable, and end up in a psychiatric hospital

What theme is running through this—people who appear mentally disturbed or shabby or having bad luck? Why does it make you so uncomfortable? Why do you get anxious even if there is no physical contact with them?

Whatever their problem it can be transferred to me. Thinking about it logically I don't believe in this stuff. It is exhausting talking about this stuff. But I know it helps and I feel better afterwards. I even have to avoid their airspace

Now, to take another example. How would you react if you saw a woman, who looks shabby and even dirty, but successful, happily talking to a group of her friends who are obviously at ease and enjoying her company? What would happen if she touched you as the group walked past?

Wouldn't bother me, might even wish to talk to her

Take it a step further. You get upset at the sight or touch of someone who is enduring misfortune, but not if they are seemingly successful, even if they are less than clean

That's right. I can pick up misfortune from homeless, disturbed people. I can even pick up the flaw that has brought them misfortune. Here we go into goof germs again

When you are out with your husband and son, do you worry that they too might pick up thought germs from weird/shabby/unstable people?

Not really

And when they are going out without you, do you worry that they might pick up the germs?

No

I wonder, why is it that they are not at risk?

Yes, it's crazy, isn't it?

Often the people who develop the sort of fear that troubles you so much come to believe that they alone are at risk, they are specially at risk. And that seems to be true for you

Yes, yes, I suppose it is. Even my family is not affected. So strange

To recap so far. The positive evidence of picking up thought germs is that proximity or contact with these people gives the same feeling of fear that you experience when you touch germ-contaminated material. On the other hand, the feeling that these people have thought germs and that they are contagious has little or no positive evidence. Health workers do not pick up mental illnesses from their patients. Your husband and child are not vulnerable to picking up the thought germs. There are no antibiotic medicines for treating mental illness. Come to that, can you think of anyone who picked up a mental illness or became mentally unstable as a result of coming into contact with people carrying thought germs?

Let's write all of this evidence on the board. How can we explain the fact that proximity makes you feel so anxious?

I think it might have something to do with my fear of mental illness; well, not mental illness exactly but more what you might call mentally unstable or weird

How long has that troubled you?

A long time

Before or after you developed a fear of contamination?

About the same time, about 16

Why did it worry you so?

That was my reputation in the family, that I was nervous and weak. A follower, not a leader

Your whole family?

Well, really my mother. My father said very little

What led her to call you nervous and weak?

I was quiet, and she said that I was easily influenced. I didn't have a mind of my own. In a way she was right. About being weak

At work, are you weak? Are you easily influenced? What is your reputation at work?

A good reputation. I am dependable, know my job well, manage my team well. I have been promoted and carry considerable responsibility

What about your husband and friends? Do they regard you as weak and easily influenced?

No, I really don't think so. I have a good marriage and my husband and I get on well. My friends? No, they treat me in the normal way that friends do. I help them, they help me. We do things together

None of this sounds to me like a person on the edge of becoming weird, does it?

No. Except for this problem of mine, with the fear

And by the way, you had an enjoyable and successful 3 years at college. No bad luck, no bad luck germs, no goof germs. There was a long period in your life when you were free of the beliefs about mind germs, and free of the fear of experiencing a serious misfortune because of proximity to unfortunate people

Yes, that's true. I really enjoyed myself at college

And during your years at college you were well and relatively untroubled by the distressing thoughts and fears—and all this without repeated washing or other rituals. Without mental neutralizing. In recent anxious years you have relied on these methods to defend yourself, but, as you say, they are not too helpful, are they?

As the didactic work and cognitive analysis proceeded the patient was encouraged to refrain from her customary avoidance of proximity to the troubling people. After six sessions of treatment, she reported some progress.

During the past month have you encountered any of the troubling, "undesirable" people?

Yes, a few. Quite a few. I am keeping it in mind

And what happened?

I felt uncomfortable, and a few times had strong urges to wash

Did you wash?

No, I managed without washing

Did you avoid any of these people?

No, I'm training myself to not avoid

Excellent. Keep it up. It's important

The urge is to get away, but I don't

In earlier conversations we talked about the basis of your fear of picking up unfortunate characteristics from these people, or of changing into them

Yes, we did

It was the bedrock of your fear of being affected by them. What is your present thinking about this, your present belief?

I no longer believe it is true. I no longer believe it can happen. I don't believe it, but just react that way

Do you now believe that you can change into such a person, or become like them in any significant way?

It is not true. Except in the movies . . .

Another reason to go to a library instead . . . It is the belief and the consequent urges to avoid and to wash yourself that promote the fear and keep it going. It appears to be related to your more obvious and familiar fears of being harmed by touching pesticides or other nasty substances. It seems that these familiar fears of being contaminated spread from nasty substances to certain people. They might spread illnesses, or immorality. It seems to me to be a form of contamination

It is the same thing. Exactly the same feeling

Are the urges similar?

Yes

Is the urge to avoid the same?

Yes it is. Well, I might become like them, mentally unstable and end up in a psychiatric hospital

The patient responded favorably to CBT. Her fear of morphing diminished, and she was increasingly able to inhibit any urges to avoid such people. Her handwashing declined to a low level. The belief that proximity to unfortunate people would harm her faded to a feeling of uneasiness that she was able to control, and she no longer felt the need to avoid their airspace. She reinterpreted the conviction that she is vulnerable to mind germs as a superstition.

As far as the morphing is concerned, her original fear was that she would become mentally unstable/weird, and this led her to avoid, and to wash compulsively. Further discussions and analysis were integrated into behavioral experiments, and a program of exposure exercises was also carried out. Initially some behavioral experiments were designed to ascertain whether her analysis of the ups and downs of the fear was consistent with her actual experiences (they were), and also to uncover any new information about the fear. Then experiments were set up to test her expectations about the consequences of planned, specific encounters with threatening and non-threatening people. She learned that the expected anxiety was evoked by closeness to threatening people, but that the anxiety gradually diminished without washing or other neutralizing acts. She also learned that the planned contacts were not followed by any changes in her personality or mental stability. After the new information was analysed she felt a decline in the fears and in her conviction that she was in danger when she encountered odd, unstable, shabby, weird people. The *current fear*, of becoming mentally unstable, was substantially reduced. Her ordinary fears of contact contamination were treated by standard ERP exercises with reasonable success.

During the assessment, her score on the CTAF scale revealed a high degree of TAF, including endorsements of these statements: "If I have a thought of a friend/relative becoming contaminated it increases the risk of them getting contaminated," "If I get an image of myself being contaminated it will make me feel contaminated." In light of this, the didactic early part of the treatment included information about the TAF phenomenon and tactics for overriding the bias.

> Before we started to talk about your fear of coming close to these people, did you make a connection between this fear and your various fears of becoming contaminated by contact with nasty substances, pesticides?

> *No, I didn't. I thought of it as just one more anxiety that was causing such difficulties in my life*

> Well, contact with these people still makes you a bit anxious—but you are no longer washing compulsively and you are no longer avoiding, even though you still get the urge occasionally. What is helping?

> *I think the non-avoiding is important, and of course the belief has gone. You assured me that people do not change in that way. It never happens. And that helped. I can't think of anyone who was changed in this way; people are never transformed into others. The sight of some of these people still makes me uneasy, but I carry on as normal—no avoiding and no more washing. I can think of the mind germs as quirky and illogical*

In this case, the nature of her fear of becoming tainted by proximity to "undesirable" people was clarified. It was explained that these fears are not delusional and the affected person knows full well that the thoughts are irrational (see Appendix 8).

Case 9.2

A 36-year-old single heterosexual male had unwanted intrusive thoughts and images of a homosexual nature. The images typically involved him engaging in sexual acts with some of his male friends. He began to wonder if these images meant that he was homosexual, and started to avoid spending time with his male friends if any sports were involved, as this usually involved changing. Following any sporting activities with his friends, he reported being plagued by images of them showering which he said was very distressing. He began to wonder if the anxiety he experienced following these images was actually a sign of sexual arousal and this exacerbated his fears.

Initially, there was no washing behavior associated with these thoughts or images and his early attempts at thought suppression were reportedly successful. However, as these grew less successful, the patient decided that one way to correct this problem was to masturbate while imagining, as vividly as possible, sexual acts with girlfriends and other women. If any thoughts or images of men intruded during this act, he would engage in compulsive washing, primarily of his hands and genitalia, often lasting for 30–45 minutes. If he was successful at precluding the images of men, no compulsive washing followed. Over time, the washing was provoked simply by the intrusive thoughts and images, regardless of whether or not he was masturbating or suppressing. When asked about this, he explained that he was trying to wash away his thoughts and images.

Treatment began with psycho-education and was followed by behavior experiments and cognitive exercises designed to provide and test alternative interpretations of his images and thoughts. This included discussion of the function of his washing behavior as well as the differences between feeling dirty and being dirty. The treatment included a small amount of exposure and response prevention. Over a period of approximately 12 sessions, his thoughts, images, and washing behavior were all dramatically reduced.

Case 9.3

Another patient with a long history of contamination fears and compulsive washing responded well to CBT but experienced an odd recurrence several years later. The feelings of contamination and associated washing returned but at lower intensity. However, in addition he had developed checking compulsions and a pervasive fear of being changed for the worse. He had become fearful of encountering people who appeared to be mentally unstable or addicted to drugs, and was even afraid that if he looked at them for too long they might hypnotize him and change him into one of them. *"If they come close to me it is a very uncomfortable feeling, maybe I'll turn into somebody like them. If they touch me I have to go and wash immediately. That usually helps, but not always. If they touch me or I touch their clothing it is scary; similar to the feelings I get if I touch garbage or chemicals, and I have to make sure that I don't spread it to the rest of my body or possessions."* His fearful beliefs about contamination, and the danger of harm being transmitted to him from unstable or unfortunate people, were not part of a delusional system and he continued to work and socialize in his customarily selective manner. He recognized that the beliefs were irrational but was unable to control them. On retreatment the fears of morphing responded favorably to cognitive methods combined with exposure exercises, but his attendance was erratic and the retreatment of the familiar contact contamination fears could not be completed.

Case 9.4

A perfectionist 28-year-old mature student had been forced to leave her studies due to the fear that she would lose her intellectual capacity ("become stupid") by coming into contact with people who were less intelligent than herself. She assessed intelligence by the person's ability to use grammar correctly and avoided people whom she feared could "turn her stupid." She had recurrent intrusive images of particular people she regarded as unintelligent, and believed that these images could contaminate the quality of her work in two ways. First, she feared that she would be so preoccupied with the images (and countering them in her head) that she would be unable to concentrate and would do poorly. This was not an unrealistic fear. Second, she feared that the images would magically influence her degree result, although she accepted this was unlikely to be the case.

The patient also avoided touching any objects (e.g., a stapler) that may have been used by "stupid" people. If forced to touch these objects she engaged in repeated tests of her intelligence, for example by making sure she fully understood a passage she was reading. These tests were repeated mental rituals involving visualizing and "working through" words. The repeated testing of her intellectual capacity was so time-consuming that she had little time for relationships or hobbies, and instead worked most of the day and night. She also avoided people who were homeless or whom she regarded as "thuggish" lest they attack her and cause a head injury that would mean she would be unable to study. One year prior to the start of her particular concerns about her intellectual capacity, she had received a diagnosis of a mild learning difficulty, and it had been suggested that she visualize words to ensure she fully understood them. Prior to treatment she did not connect the diagnosis of a learning disability with the onset of her obsessive behavior.

The patient received 15 sessions of treatment which encouraged her to take the default position that she understood what she was reading or hearing without having to test herself. A distinction was drawn between "emotional understanding" and "intellectual understanding." She was encouraged to allow the images to enter her head and then continue to work without engaging in neutralizing behavior. The patient agreed to come into contact with people and objects she regarded as "stupid" and was able to do this relatively easily. She was able to conclude from this and behavior tests and surveys that her unwanted images of people and contact with them did not affect her intellectual performance. She was much improved after treatment.

Chapter 10

Visual Contamination

There is a connection between visual contamination and morphing. In most instances of the fear of morphing the person becomes sensitive to visual contamination. The mere sight of an "undesirable" person evokes the fear.

There are some similarities between visual contamination and beliefs in magical thinking. Frazer (1922), an authority on magical thinking, set out two principles of sympathetic magic. Influence at a distance is inherent in the second of the two principles—the law of similarity, in which "like produces like": a "magical sympathy exists between a man and any . . . portion of his person—whoever gets possession of human hair or nails may work his will, at any distance, upon the person from whom they were cut" (p.43). According to the law of similarity, enemies can be harmed at a distance by damaging them in effigy or by damaging their possessions (hair, nails, clothing). People can be psychologically harmed even at a distance, visually—as in cases of a fear of morphing.

The law of contagion states that "things which have once been in contact continue ever afterwards to act on each other" (Frazer, 1922, p.12), even if all physical contact has ended. They continue to influence each other even at a distance. The continuing magical contact can be threatening and the affected person therefore attempts to remove all traces of the connection by washing and/or by carrying out purification rituals. The resemblance of the law of contagion to the non-degradable quality of contamination described in Chapter 1 is notable: once in contact always in contact.

If all or most contacts with contaminated materials, places, or people continue to exert their influence even when further physical contact is avoided, and if the influences operate at a distance, this can lead to an expanding contagion of contamination; people can be harmed at a distance (Rachman, 2006). Feelings of visual contamination, so common in cases of a fear of morphing, are consistent with the observation that the influence of "things which have once been in contact" will continue to be in contact, even at a distance. Visual contamination at a distance persists.

10.1 **Treatment of visual contamination**

The treatment of visual contamination proceeds from a cognitive analysis of the person's current anxiety. Treatment usually includes behavior experiments designed to test whether visual exposure to the people concerned does in fact lead to the acquisition of their undesirable characteristics or whether the exposures actually damage one's stable personality characteristics. Following the information gathered in these experiments patients are encouraged to inhibit their extensive avoidance of situations where they anticipate seeing people who will make them feel polluted or contaminated. Rescripting of disturbing intrusive images, focused on the visual cues for contamination, is an effective technique for overcoming the distressing intrusions. When the visual contamination is associated with a fear of morphing, successful treatment of the morphing is generally followed by the extinction of the visual sensitivity.

There are cases of visual contamination that are not associated with a fear of morphing, and they are treated by cognitive analyses, rescripting of images, and behavior experiments.

Visual contamination is so frequently evident in the fear of morphing that the treatment focuses primarily on the morphing. When the contamination arises from the sight of a violator, people associated with the violator, or a person who resembles the violator in appearance or manner, the treatment focuses on extinguishing the effects of the violation. In one case the feelings of contamination were evoked by the sight of any member of the violator's very large family.

Case illustrations of treatment of visual contamination

Case 10.1

A student, Robert, who developed a fear of contamination after being threatened by three drunk, dishevelled, aggressive men while walking home from a late-night movie, was referred for CBT. He had wandered into a rough area where he was accosted by the men who demanded his money. One of them grabbed his jacket and threatened to beat him. The patient managed to leave the area, poorer but physically unharmed. He was extremely upset by the incident and felt so dirty that on arriving home he took a long hot shower. He ruminated about the incident and became so frightened of street people that he scanned his surroundings intensively and avoided any place that had associations with the violating event. The mere sight of a potentially intimidating person, even at a distance, contaminated him. On those occasions when his avoidant behavior was unsuccessful he was driven to wash compulsively.

The therapy combined an analysis of his frightening cognitions, including fears about his mental stability, and graded exposure exercises to the people and places that evoked his fear and contamination. He benefitted significantly from 15 sessions of CBT spread over 1 year. However, he experienced a partial return of fear 2 years later and required four booster sessions.

Case 10.2

A young girl developed a habit of intense repeated blinking in an attempt to clean her mind by washing away the threat of becoming a drug addict or a helpless homeless person. The blinking occurred whenever she saw a shabby-looking, disreputable street person, and her parents observed that the blinking was particularly intense whenever the family drove past a rundown part of the city. She responded well to CBT and advice to resist the urges to blink because they were misdirected and not helpful. It was explained to her and her parents that the sight of the disreputable people would not and could not harm her health or personality, and that the repetitive blinking was slightly embarrassing and no longer necessary. They were advised that it was neither necessary nor advisable to plan their journeys in order to avoid the sight of shabby-looking and apparently disreputable people.

Chapter 11

Case Series

In a clinical case series, CBT was effective for 9 out of 12 patients diagnosed with mental contamination (Coughtrey et al., 2012b). The average Obsessive-Compulsive Inventory-Revised (OCI-R) (Foa et al., 2002) score at the start of treatment was 42, indicating that patients had OCD of moderate to severe severity (Foa et al., 2002). All patients had failed to respond to some form of psychological intervention for their OCD symptoms in the past (nine had received a course of CBT incorporating ERP) and four participants were receiving pharmacological treatment for their OCD at the start of treatment. No participant initiated or continued in another form of psychological or pharmacological therapy during treatment or follow-up.

Patients received between 10 and 20 treatment sessions of 50 minutes duration. Participants attended a research assessment prior to the intervention and at the end of treatment and were contacted approximately 3 months and 6 months after the last treatment session to obtain follow-up data.

11.1 Outcomes

Eight patients completed a 3-month follow-up and seven completed a 6-month follow-up. Following treatment, 7 out of 12 patients no longer met the diagnostic criteria for OCD. These gains were maintained at follow-up. The remaining five patients still met the diagnostic criteria for OCD; two of these patients no longer experienced mental contamination. Table 11.1 shows the scores for each patient at pre-treatment, post-treatment, and follow-up. Follow-up data are missing for five patients. Patients who demonstrated clinically significant change are highlighted in italics (Jacobson and Truax, 1991).

Table 11.1 Psychometric scores pre- and post-treatment and at follow-up. Patients who demonstrated clinically significant change are highlighted in italics

Patient number	P1	P2	P3	P4	P5	P6	P7	P8	P9	P10	P11	P12	Mean
Patient age	34	19	29	44	22	22	22	43	25	31	21	34	
Patient gender	F	M	M	M	F	M	F	F	F	F	M	F	
YBOCS (total) Pre-treatment	29	29	30	34	27	33	29	32	21	28	26	29	29
Post-treatment	6	32	1	35	22	2	1	28	3	24	3	2	13.42
3-month follow-up	3	–	0	–	–	2	1	27	1	–	2	1	12.75
6-month follow-up	4	–	4	–	–	0	1	–	2	–	1	1	12.92
VOCI-MC Pre-treatment	68	41	45	94	52	40	52	74	46	55	59	59	57.92
Post-treatment	13	15	5	83	49	2	8	76	3	15	4	6	24
3-month follow-up	7	–	3	–	–	0	9	75	4	–	1	5	22.92
6-month follow-up	8	–	4	–	–	4	8	–	2	–	11	8	24.25
OCI-R Pre-treatment	45	34	55	56	27	31	36	64	46	28	37	42	42.67
Post-treatment	12	35	5	42	18	8	5	39	4	16	10	6	18.25
3-month follow-up	10	–	6	–	–	11	7	42	6	–	3	5	18.33
6-month follow-up	10	–	8	–	–	12	9	–	5	–	4	6	18.83

Paired sample t-tests revealed significant group reductions for all the measures pre- to post-treatment: YBOCS, $t(11) = 4.17$, $p = 0.002$, $d = 1.55$; OCI-R, $t(11) = 5.42$, $p < 0.001$, $d = 1.84$; VOCI-MC, $t(11) = 5.94$, $p < 0.001$, $d = 1.42$.

Case 11.1

Natalia was a woman in her 30s who felt internally dirty and washed her hands after experiencing unwanted intrusive thoughts and images, following conflict with someone, or if she stood near to someone whom she considered to be morally dubious. She also believed that her feelings of internal dirtiness could transfer to objects and feared that she may contaminate her son with her thoughts. As a result she washed her hands in excess of 80 times per day, insisted her son regularly wash his hands, spent 5 hours per day cleaning her house, regularly changed her and her son's clothes throughout the day, and had clothes specifically for outside wear to avoid the spread of mind germs. In addition, when she experienced a negative thought she felt compelled to repeat her current action while replacing the negative thought with a positive one in order to prevent the action from becoming tainted and bringing "bad luck" for ever more. Prior to treatment her symptoms were having a detrimental emotional impact on her life; she often felt angry, frustrated, and guilty and felt that her behavior was damaging her relationship with her young son, family, and friends.

Natalia had previously completed six sessions of group therapy for OCD which she had found helpful, but remained significantly impaired. At assessment she reported low mood and suicidal ideation but was not actively suicidal. Treatment focused on her contamination-related cognitive bias (TAF) and involved numerous behavioral experiments with Natalia's family to challenge beliefs about the nature and spread of contamination, and the influence of thoughts on the occurrence of negative events and physical illness. Experimenting with "doing things differently" was helpful for Natalia to test her beliefs surrounding her ability to cope with her contamination fears. Following 15 sessions of CBT, Natalia no longer met the diagnostic criteria for OCD or any other mental health problem. She was able to let clothes be worn twice before being washed, and washed her hands only before preparing food and after using the toilet. She no longer washed her son's hands or changed his clothes unnecessarily. These changes were maintained at 3 and 6 months follow-up.

Case 11.2

Henry was a man in his late-teens who presented with a 4-year history of compulsive handwashing triggered by doubts about coming into contact with dangerous and disgusting substances, and obsessions about vandalizing, and hurting people. These thoughts and images would leave Henry with feelings of dirtiness on his hands and feet that compelled him to wash compulsively. In addition, Henry would "check" mental images of himself to ensure that he was free of contamination and had not caused harm to anyone. Henry's OCD symptoms were significantly interfering with his life; he was unable to work because of his difficulties and felt that it was having a detrimental impact on his personal relationships. Henry had completed eight sessions of group therapy for OCD and six sessions of individual CBT prior to assessment. In addition, at the start of treatment he had been taking 100 mg fluoxetine daily at a stable dose for the past 12 months.

Henry completed 12 sessions of individual CBT that focused on his assumptions that he had done something bad or dangerous. Examining the link between concern over causing harm and feeling dirty was particularly important in formulating this patient's difficulties and establishing what caused the sensations on his hands and feet. Therapy focused on the meaning of dirt and Henry attempted to "act as if" he was not contaminated unless he knew that he was. Although Henry was initially able to complete these experimental tasks he found it difficult to maintain the changes and extrapolate them to his everyday life due to his low self-esteem and a lack of self-efficacy. He showed a reduction in his mental contamination symptoms and washing behavior at post-treatment but still met the criteria for a diagnosis of OCD. The reasons for Henry's minimal improvement included a lack of self-efficacy and self-esteem as indicated by his belief that there was little point in his implementing changes because (i) he did not believe that he could and (ii) he did not think that he would be able to influence his OCD anyway. At the end of treatment, Henry was referred for treatment for his low self-esteem.

Case 11.3

Kiran was a man in his late 20s who was referred for treatment of an excessive fear of contracting HIV or hepatitis in the absence of physical contact with any potential pollutant. Kiran was frightened that he might inadvertently pass on this contamination to his family and therefore he would engage in repeated checking to ensure that contamination would not spread. He reported significant TAF in that he felt able to prevent bad things from happening and had bad numbers that would leave him with feelings of foreboding and dirtiness that could only be neutralized with good numbers. Kiran had previously received two sessions of CBT for his OCD symptoms, which had developed when he was around 7 years of age.

He completed ten sessions of treatment during which he made excellent progress. CTAF was the main focus of treatment and involved extensive behavioral experiments during which Kiran deliberately tried to get contaminated and cause harm to others, whilst reducing avoidance and deliberately leaving tasks on a bad number. These experiments allowed Kiran to challenge his belief that he would feel contaminated forever; in fact he found that his feelings of contamination, guilt, and anxiety reduced quite rapidly by themselves. At the end of treatment, he no longer met the diagnostic criteria for OCD or experienced mental contamination. These gains were maintained at 3 and 6 months follow-up.

Case 11.4

Sanjeev was a man in his 40s who presented with extreme contamination fear. His OCD symptoms had begun in his early 20s when he began to attempt to neutralize unwanted blasphemous thoughts. Sanjeev experienced unwanted intrusive sexual thoughts which left him feeling extremely contaminated and with strong urges to wash and clean his hands 18 times over. His feelings of mental pollution were so severe that he needed to spit out food if he had a bad thought while eating. He regularly cleaned himself with bleach and scraped his skin with a razor blade in an attempt to remove his contaminated skin. Sanjeev's symptoms had a detrimental impact upon his work and social functioning. He was unable to work and avoided holding his daughter for fear of contaminating her. As a result, his relationship with his wife was under considerable strain. In addition, Sanjeev reported panic attacks, severe depression, and suicidal ideation. Prior to starting treatment he was taking citalopram (20 mg) augmented with clonazepam (100 mg), and diazepam (5 mg) on a *pro re nata* basis. His medication dosages were stable.

Sanjeev completed 20 sessions of CBT over which he made limited progress. Intrusive sexual images were particularly relevant for Sanjeev, and therapy included psycho-education and surveys to gather information about unwanted sexual images and behavioral experiments to test Sanjeev's beliefs about contamination from sexual thoughts. These included "Theory A vs. Theory B" contrast experiments and experiments to reduce washing and reassurance seeking. The results of these behavioral experiments allowed Sanjeev to stop spitting food out when he had unwanted intrusive thoughts, reduce the shaving of his skin, and allow his sexual images to come through. The remaining sessions of treatment tackled Sanjeev's low mood, suicidal ideation, anger, and marital difficulties. He was angry with his partner and had previously got into physical fights in public places with strangers. His anger and low mood combined made some aspects of treatment such as behavioral experiments particularly challenging. At the end of treatment he still met the diagnostic criteria for OCD and experienced severe mental contamination concerns. In addition, Sanjeev's depression had worsened in severity and he was experiencing strong suicidal ideation. Sanjeev was referred for in-patient treatment.

Case 11.5

Guen was a woman in her 20s who presented with unwanted intrusive thoughts and images about harming others. Guen believed that these intrusions meant that she was immoral, that the thoughts were revealing her true character, and that she could be morphing into a murderer. She engaged in mental rituals which involved imagining the scenario and asking questions about whether she could harm someone and her emotional reactions to it. She reported that she could only stop this mental process when it "felt right" and she would then telephone her family for reassurance.

Guen completed six sessions of treatment during which she started to make adequate progress regarding the contaminating effect that her unwanted intrusive images had on her sense of self. Treatment also involved cognitive analyses to establish how Guen would determine that she was turning into a murderer and a behavioral experiment where she actively tried to transform herself into someone else. Although Guen had made adequate progress she terminated treatment after the sixth session as she was moving out of the area.

Case 11.6

Mike was a man in his 20s whose contamination fears centred on a fear of contaminating the future by inviting "badness" into his life. Although he did not present with excessive washing behavior, he often felt compelled to take sips of water in response to his obsessions. Mike reported being unable to sleep for longer than 1 hour at a time and was unable to eat regularly because of his unwanted intrusive thoughts, and in addition would often delete portions of written work because of a fear that something bad would happen in the future. Mike experienced periods of severe low mood lasting several days during which he felt unable to complete everyday tasks. Mike had received five sessions of counseling to address his anxiety, which he felt had had limited benefit, and had self-prescribed *Ginkgo biloba* which he had been taking for 2 months in an attempt to control his obsessive thoughts.

Treatment focused on developing his feelings of self-efficacy and coping strategies for stress to ease Mike's low mood, before targeting beliefs about CTAF. This involved a number of surveys to gather information about "normal" superstitious beliefs and consultation with a number of specialists, including a sleep expert and a Muslim authority figure. Mike was then able to complete a number of behavioral experiments to test his beliefs about contamination based around a "Theory A vs. Theory B" comparison. Mike completed 14 sessions of CBT during which he made excellent progress. At the end of treatment Mike no longer met the criteria for OCD, had significantly improved mood, and reported normal sleeping and eating routines, i.e., sleeping 7–8 hours per night and eating three meals a day. These gains were maintained at 3 and 6 months follow-up.

Case 11.7

Jenny was a woman in her 20s who presented with a fear of morphing. Specifically, she felt dirty from being near immoral people and reported feeling vicariously guilty, as if she herself had done something wrong. For Jenny, dirty feelings were akin to feelings of shame and guilt. Being near these undesirable people would leave her feeling dirty under her skin and left her with an urge to drink water and to shower. These feelings of pollution and urges to wash could also be provoked by unwanted intrusive thoughts and images about abusing children and incest. Jenny had received eight sessions of individual CBT for her OCD 3 years previously (the content of which was not similar to evidence-based CBT recommended by the National Institute for Health and Care Excellence (NICE)), but which she had found partially beneficial. However, she had relapsed following a personal betrayal 6 months previously. At assessment she was taking 30 mg of citalopram daily, at a stable dose for 5.5 months.

Jenny completed ten sessions of treatment during which she made excellent progress. The therapy focused on testing her beliefs about morals, guilt, and the omission/commission bias (e.g., Wroe and Salkovskis, 2000). She found that rewriting her moral standards modeled on her grandmother's was particularly helpful in making them more realistic. These standards were then used in "old mindset/new mindset" experiments. Jenny also conducted behavioral experiments in which she deliberately tried to cause harm to others, and contrast experiments to reduce her washing and neutralizing behavior. From session 6 onwards Jenny began to reduce her anti-depressant medication dose. At the end of treatment she no longer required medication and did not meet the diagnostic criteria for mental contamination or any mental health problem. These gains were maintained at 3 and 6 months follow-up.

Case 11.8

Zoe was a 43-year-old woman with an 18-year history of OCD symptoms related to a fear of contamination associated with feces. Zoe demonstrated mental contamination in that even imagining feces would cause her to feel dirty and wash compulsively. For Zoe, the term dirty was associated with being pathetic and useless, resulting from an unhappy marriage during which she endured physical violence and humiliation. At the beginning of treatment, Zoe reported excessive washing behavior including using two bottles of shower gel per day, and double washing all her clothes using five washing tablets per wash. Zoe had not slept in her own bed for over 10 years for fear of spreading contamination. Related to her contamination fears, Zoe presented with low mood, low self-esteem, and frequent panic attacks. She had received individual CBT for her contamination fears on two previous occasions, once for 14 sessions and another for 16 sessions.

Zoe completed 14 sessions of treatment during which she made some improvement with regard to her contamination fear. Discussion of betrayal and humiliation was particularly important with Zoe, in order to establish that the term dirty was associated with being pathetic and useless. Treatment involved cognitive analyses and behavioral experiments to demonstrate that feelings of humiliation and betrayal could make her feel dirty. Similarly, cognitive techniques were used to allow Zoe to reinterpret the significance of the feelings of contamination, to address the meaning of dirtiness, and to separate anger, aversion, and feeling pathetic and useless from feelings of contamination. An aim of the cognitive analyses was to establish that there were other and preferable ways to feel better other than needing to feel clean. Zoe also completed a number of tasks to improve her self-esteem. By the end of treatment Zoe had made some significant improvements; for example, she was able to sleep in her own bed.

However, she still met the diagnostic criteria for OCD and continued to experience crippling contamination fears. She was referred for psychotherapy and work on her self-esteem problems.

Case 11.9

Safiya was a woman in her mid-20s who presented with a wide range of difficulties with contamination, including a strong fear that she may harm vulnerable people such as the elderly or people whom she cared about by inadvertently spreading germs and illnesses such as hepatitis. Safiya also presented with symptoms of mental contamination, as she reported that she sometimes feared that simply being in close proximity to a contaminated item could cause contamination to spread. Similarly, even thinking about spreading contamination left Safiya feeling dirty and generated an urge to wash. These contamination fears generated extreme anticipatory anxiety and guilt, and in response Safiya reported washing her hands in excess of 50 times a day. She showered in a ritualized and excessive way, using anti-bacterial soap, and when the feelings of contamination were particularly severe, Safiya felt compelled to throw away her contaminated possessions. Safiya had previously completed 12 sessions of individual CBT but had not found it beneficial in reducing her contamination fear.

Treatment focused on anticipatory guilt and how this increased her feelings of responsibility, immorality, and internal pollution and mental contamination. Therapy included addressing the probability of harm, responsibility pie charts, and considering the role of anticipation and attention. In addition, Safiya completed a number of behavioral experiments including "acting as if" she had not caused harm, reducing washing and showering behaviors, and attempting to transfer harm by sending greetings cards to vulnerable people.

Over the course of the 12 sessions of treatment Safiya made excellent progress, and at the end of treatment she no longer met the diagnostic criteria for any mental health problem. These gains were maintained at 3 and 6 months follow-up.

Case 11.10

Emma was a woman in her 30s who reported that unwanted aggressive intrusive thoughts, images of being sexually assaulted, and memories of times when she had previously felt very dirty could make her feel contaminated and trigger an urge to wash. She also felt dirty if she stood next to certain people and reported feeling like she had somehow "caught" their dirtiness. Emma showered and washed her hair twice a day, shampooing two to three times per wash. She also reported excessive washing of her two young children. Emma attended the initial two treatment sessions (assessment and formulation) during which she made good progress of grasping the CBT model. However, she felt unable to attend any further sessions because of her home and work commitments.

Case 11.11

Ahmet was a young man in his 20s who reported excessive washing in an attempt to "anti-bacterialize" everything, including himself. This resulted from a fear of physical germs causing illness and preventing him from working, but also from a fear of "mind germs." He reported feelings of mental contamination in that he would need to shower after experiencing an unwanted immoral thought, having a bad dream, or experiencing some form of negative criticism. He felt dirty and contaminated in the presence of people whom he considered dirty or immoral and feared that homeless or mentally ill people could contaminate him and he could become like them. This would be triggered even if he did not come into physical contact with them. After a contact of this kind, Ahmet would wash his hands in a highly ritualized way and pick his skin to remove contamination. In the past Ahmet had received two sessions of supportive counseling and had been taking 50 mg fluoxetine daily.

Ahmet completed ten sessions of treatment which focused on lowering his feelings of moral responsibility and moral TAF. Ahmet completed a number of contrast experiments to reduce his avoidance of immoral people and to reduce his neutralizing behavior (washing, aligning and counting, and wearing pale-colored clothes). By doing this, Ahmet was able to recognize that when he did not respond to his intrusive thoughts or dreams his anxiety declined and he did not catch "mind germs." Ahmet made excellent progress and at the end of treatment was free of medication and no longer met the criteria for any mental health disorder. These gains were maintained at 3 and 6 months follow-up.

Case 11.12

Caroline was a woman in her 40s with a 27-year history of contamination concerns and compulsive washing. Caroline's OCD symptoms centered on preventing harm to herself and her loved ones, which led her to repeat actions when she had a bad thought and to replace bad thoughts with positive ones in order to prevent the bad thought traveling with her and contaminating other people and items. She described feeling as if she had badness all over her skin and feared she could transmit the badness to others via her thoughts, although she had good insight that this thinking was magical. She also reported having a number of mental shields which she used to protect herself, her possessions, and her loved ones from badness. In addition, Caroline reported that she had a particular vulnerability to turning into people whom she perceived to be undesirable. She reported washing herself and her clothes if she came into contact with these people or omens. She also reported an inability to discuss the future, as she felt that she might contaminate it, and by discussing it would be inviting something bad to happen. Caroline had received six sessions of individual CBT in the past but had found it of minimal use.

Caroline completed 16 sessions of treatment during which she made excellent progress. Initially, the main focus of treatment was addressing Caroline's beliefs about contaminating the future through a series of surveys and behavioral experiments. This work enabled Caroline to establish that the problem was not that she could contaminate the future but that it was a problem of her thinking. The focus of the remaining sessions was on Caroline's mental shield that she had constructed to cope with her feelings of mental contamination.

Monitoring her shield and conducting an experiment within a treatment session enabled her to realize that rather than protecting her from feeling contaminated, constructing the shield maintained her focus on her feelings of contamination and thus prolonged her anxiety and feelings of pollution. As a result of this, Caroline began to conduct behavioral experiments in which she would come into contact with places, people, and objects that she had previously avoided, both with and without using her shield. Over time, she was able to use the mental image of the shield less, and this allowed her to significantly reduce her avoidance. The final stage of treatment tackled Caroline's beliefs about social judgments and her feeling of being vulnerable to morphing because of her unstable sense of self. General cognitive and behavioral techniques to improve self-esteem were used, and Caroline started to generate a list of things that she felt was stable about her sense of self. Caroline was introduced to formal problem-solving techniques to enable her to strengthen the feeling that she had the capacity to cope and deal with negative life events.

At the end of treatment Caroline no longer met the diagnostic criteria for any mental health problem. She no longer avoided large areas of her local town and was able to talk freely about the future and have physical contact with her loved ones. These gains were maintained at 3 and 6 months follow-up.

The findings from this case series indicate that mental contamination is responsive to CBT treatment. Those patients who were able successfully to engage in the cognitive analyses, especially the "contrasting comparisons" of Explanation A vs. Explanation B, carry out the behavioral experiments, and adapt them where necessary made the greatest gains in treatment. Two patients completed treatment but did not show any clinically significant improvement in mental contamination or OCD symptoms. The reasons for lack of progress in these two cases included severe depression, suicidality, and low self-esteem, which made it difficult for these patients to apply what they learned in the sessions to their home environments. It is noteworthy that these patients had experienced symptoms of mental contamination for a considerable length of time, and both had received CBT for their OCD on more than one occasion in the past. In addition, they had the highest scores on the mental contamination scale at the start of treatment, and one patient presented with co-morbid panic disorder. These findings suggest that people with long-standing complex mental contamination may benefit from a lengthier or different approach to treatment. Alternatively it may be preferable to address co-morbid problems, such as persisting depression, prior to treating the mental contamination.

Chapter 12

Implications of Cognitive Behavioral Therapy for Mental Contamination

Recognition of the nature and occurrence of the phenomenon of mental contamination enables clinicians to detect this important manifestation of OCD. The provision of methods of assessment, standardized interviews, probes of imagery, and validated psychometric tests facilitates detection and the monitoring of the disorder.

In view of the insufficiency of the prevailing treatment for OCD, many patients suffering from mental contamination continue to suffer. We anticipate that the provision of the cognitive therapy designed to deal specifically with this disorder will bring relief and benefit to those people whose fear of contamination is not adequately assessed. The results of therapy should improve appreciably.

Bearing in mind a weakness of early cognitive theories of anxiety disorders, the work on mental contamination moved from general propositions to increasingly specific analyses, explanations, and treatment methods. Given the evidence that cognitions can produce and maintain feelings of mental contamination, the approach has focused on cognitive assessments and explanations. This is a significant shift in emphasis away from behavioral explanations and treatment tactics to cognitive explanations, assessments, and treatments.

The close connection between theory and therapy is a strength of cognitive clinical psychology, and is evident in the therapy developed for dealing with mental contamination. The therapy is deduced from the theory. Cognitive models of anxiety disorders have provided a platform for the derivation of specific methods of treatment (e.g., Beck, 1976; D.M. Clark, 1986; D.A. Clark and Beck, 2011; Salkovskis, 1985; Rachman, 1997a).

The recognition that a large proportion of OCD patients suffer from feelings of mental contamination may help to explain the disappointing results of prevailing treatment and promote better directed treatments. Jacobi et al. (2014) found that of the 122 OCD patients who participated in two successive randomized control treatment trials at their Anxiety Disorders Clinic, only 16.2% of those with a fear of contamination showed clinically significant improvements. Across the two trials, 51(43.2%) out of a total of 118 patients with OCD met the criteria for improved clinical status. Regrettably only 2 out of 20 of the patients with a fear of contamination who received group CBT were clinically improved, and of the 17 who received ERP treatment, just four attained the status of significant clinical improvement. Recently, van Balkom et al. (2012) reported that 48 of 118 patients "treated with 12 weeks of ERP, appeared to be nonresponders" (p. 336). In some trials the number of responders is higher, but the overall success rate for OCD patients hovers around 50–60%.

It is a concern that the overall success rates have not improved during the past 25 years and the drop-out and refusal rates are high. The results of a multi-site trial (Foa et al., 2005) are not appreciably different from the success rates achieved in the first randomized control study, reported 36 years ago (Rachman et al., 1979). Significant numbers of patients are unable/unwilling to undertake this demanding treatment (Arntz et al., 2007; Foa et al., 2005). According to D.A. Clark and Beck (2011) 37% of OCD patients refuse, drop out, or fail to improve. Yet others are able to carry out the necessary exposure exercises with the therapist at the clinic or hospital but are unable to do so at home. The long-term effects of behavioral treatment of OCD are less than satisfactory. "The average patient . . . continues to experience mild to moderate OC symptoms upon termination" (Eddy et al., 2004, p. 1025), and O'Sullivan and Marks (1991) reported that even after relatively successful treatment, 40% of the initial symptoms were still evident at long-term follow-up.

In the course of developing methods for treating mental contamination, we found a number of techniques to be particularly helpful alone or in combination. Optimally, these strategies are derived from the case formulation and tied closely to the theory of mental contamination. The primary goal of these strategies is to assist the patient to reinterpret the personal significance of the violation and/or the violator. Treatment is successful when a conceptual orientation takes place, as evidenced by new ways of thinking about and perceiving the contamination-related person and circumstances. The techniques include imagery rescripting, behavioral experiments, the modification of cognitive biases, relabeling emotional experiences, and a focus on current threat. Cognitive biases such as TAF, responsibility biases, and *ex-consequentia* biases are treated by cognitive analyses and the provision of corrective information, supplemented by behavior experiments. Patients who are prone to these troubling cognitive biases try to block the intrusions if they can, and suppress them if they can't. Their attempts at coping are seldom satisfactory and may even exacerbate matters (D.A. Clark, 2004; Rassin, 2006). Despite the tenacity of cognitive biases, including TAF, useful steps have been made in tackling the problem. It is important to investigate the effectiveness of these techniques, separately and jointly through experiments and clinical research endeavors. In the interim, clinicians are encouraged to use these strategies with their patients, ideally collecting evidence about their effectiveness through the course of their work. Attention is given to analysing why the patient feels under current threat. A crucial aim of treatment is to facilitate a benign realistic reappraisal of the violating events and violator.

The phenomenon of mental contamination is complex and intriguing, and as is evident from this text there are many gaps in the current knowledge to invite the curiosity of clinical researchers. One advance is the recognition that many OCD patients have enhanced memory in specifiable circumstances (Radomsky and Rachman, 1999). The significance of this finding is that several accounts of OCD assume that patients with OCD suffer from a biological deficit of memory. The research on mental contamination contradicts that broad assumption.

The four fundamental features of contamination fears—rapid acquisition, non-degradability, wide and rapid spread, asymmetry—are separately and jointly worthy of further research. Other tempting research topics include: the interplay between mental contamination and contact contamination, how to unwind cognitive biases, how to help patients brake the rapid expansion of their feelings of contamination, and investigating the basis of a heightened sensitivity to contamination. The judicious use of safety behavior needs further development for therapeutic purposes.

Some patients try to defend themselves by developing protective mental shields or "bubbles," as in the case of our patient who constructed an imaginary blue shield to protect himself from harmful intrusions invading his mind. It is a strange and fascinating phenomenon, and not unknown to the ancient Greeks. They knew that protection from danger can be provided by creating a magical shield or "bubble." On his long, hazardous journey home when Odysseus entered an unfamiliar hostile land his protector, the formidable goddess Athene, enveloped "a magic mist around her favourite in her concern for his safety" (Homer, 2003 edn, p. 86).

It is an extremely inviting subject. However, our few exploratory attempts to assist patients develop a protective screen, bubble, or mist have met with scant success so far. This particular type of judicious safety behavior is beyond our present resources.

We anticipate that the provision of the cognitive therapy designed to deal specifically with this disorder will bring relief and benefit to those people whose fear of contamination is not adequately assessed.

The need for RCTs to evaluate the effects of the cognitive treatment is evident. Positive results would require systematic dissemination of the methods and lead to ready provision of help for people afflicted by mental contamination. In addition to the need for RCTs to evaluate the therapy, it is essential that research must be dedicated to testing the main premises of the cognitive theory of mental contamination.

Part 3

Toolkit: Appendices

VOCI (Contact) Contamination Subscale Items

1 I feel very dirty after touching money.

2 I use an excessive amount of disinfectants to keep my home and myself safe from germs.

3 I spend far too much time washing my hands.

4 Touching the bottom of my shoes makes me very anxious.

5 I find it very difficult to touch garbage or garbage bins.

6 I am excessively concerned about germs and disease.

7 I avoid using public telephones because of possible contamination.

8 I feel very contaminated if I touch an animal.

9 I am afraid of having even slight contact with bodily secretions (blood, urine, sweat, etc.).

10 One of my major problems is that I am excessively concerned about cleanliness.

11 I often experience upsetting and unwanted thoughts about illness.

12 I am afraid to use even well-kept public toilets because I am so concerned about germs.

(Each item is rated as *not at all* (0), *a little* (1), *some* (2), *much* (3), or *very much* (4). The total score for this contamination subscale is the sum of the scores of all of the items.)

VOCI Mental Contamination Scale (VOCI-MC)

Please rate the extent to which you agree with the following statements	Not at all	A little	Some	Much	Very much
1. Often I look clean but feel dirty.	0	1	2	3	4
2. Having an unpleasant image or memory can make me feel dirty inside.	0	1	2	3	4
3. Often I cannot get clean no matter how thoroughly I wash myself.	0	1	2	3	4
4. If someone says something nasty to me it can make me feel dirty.	0	1	2	3	4
5. Certain people make me feel dirty or contaminated even without any direct contact.	0	1	2	3	4
6. I often feel dirty under my skin.	0	1	2	3	4
7. Some people look clean, but feel dirty.	0	1	2	3	4
8. I often feel dirty or contaminated even though I haven't touched anything dirty.	0	1	2	3	4
9. Often when I feel dirty or contaminated, I also feel guilty or ashamed.	0	1	2	3	4
10. I often experience unwanted and upsetting thoughts about dirtiness.	0	1	2	3	4
11. Some objects look clean, but feel dirty.	0	1	2	3	4

Please rate the extent to which you agree with the following statements	Not at all	A little	Some	Much	Very much
12. I often feel dirty or contaminated without knowing why.	0	1	2	3	4
13. Often when I feel dirty or contaminated, I also feel angry.	0	1	2	3	4
14. Unwanted and repugnant thoughts often make me feel contaminated or dirty.	0	1	2	3	4
15. Standing close to certain people makes me feel dirty and/or contaminated.	0	1	2	3	4
16. I often feel dirty inside my body.	0	1	2	3	4
17. If I experience certain unwanted repugnant thoughts, I need to wash myself.	0	1	2	3	4
18. Certain people or places that make me feel dirty or contaminated leave everyone else completely unaffected.	0	1	2	3	4
19. The possibility that my head will be filled with worries about contamination makes me very anxious.	0	1	2	3	4
20. I often feel the need to cleanse my mind.	0	1	2	3	4

Note: the three new scales to measure aspects of mental contamination—the Mental Contamination Scale, the Contamination Sensitivity Scale, and the Contamination Thought–Action Fusion Scale—have undergone preliminary validation and associated investigations in participants diagnosed with OCD, anxious controls, and a large group of undergraduate student participants. The results of the initial psychometric studies are encouraging (Radomsky et al., 2014). See Chapter 5 for more information about these new scales.

Mental Contamination Scale, clinical cut-off score

A clinical cut-off score for the Mental Contamination Interview of 39 correctly classified 98% of patients with significant mental contamination.

Appendix 3

Contamination Thought–Action Fusion Scale

Do you *disagree* or *agree* with the following statements?	Strongly disagree	Disagree	Neutral	Agree	Strongly agree
1. If I have a thought about a friend/relative getting ill, it increases the risk that he/she will actually get ill.	0	1	2	3	4
2. If I get an image of myself being contaminated, it will make me feel contaminated.	0	1	2	3	4
3. If I have a thought of a friend/relative becoming contaminated, it increases the risk of him/her getting contaminated.	0	1	2	3	4
4. If I have a thought about myself getting ill, it increases the risk that I will get ill.	0	1	2	3	4
5. If I have a thought about getting contaminated, it increases the risk of actually becoming contaminated.	0	1	2	3	4
6. If I have a thought that I might pass on contamination to a child, it increases the risk that the child will become contaminated.	0	1	2	3	4
7. Having a thought that I might pass contamination on to someone else is almost as bad as actually doing it.	0	1	2	3	4
8. If I get an image of a friend/relative being contaminated, it will increase the risk that he/she will actually become contaminated.	0	1	2	3	4
9. If I have a thought that I might pass on contamination to a child, that is almost as bad as actually passing it on.	0	1	2	3	4

Appendix 4

Contamination Sensitivity Scale

Do you *disagree* or *agree* with the following statements?	Strongly disagree	Disagree	Neutral	Agree	Strongly agree
1. It scares me when my hands feel sticky.	0	1	2	3	4
2. When there is something wrong with my stomach, I worry that I might be seriously ill.	0	1	2	3	4
3. It scares me when I feel dirty *inside* my body.	0	1	2	3	4
4. I can always smell if there is something rotting.	0	1	2	3	4
5. It is always important for me to wash myself absolutely clean.	0	1	2	3	4
6. If I cannot get rid of worries about contamination, I am nervous that I might be going crazy.	0	1	2	3	4
7. Touching clothing that belongs to someone I strongly dislike would make me feel nervous.	0	1	2	3	4
8. Eating fruit or vegetables that are not organic makes me feel tense and nervous.	0	1	2	3	4
9. I keep well away from people who look ill.	0	1	2	3	4
10. For me, unpleasant smells are extremely nauseating.	0	1	2	3	4
11. It scares me if I feel dirty *under* my skin.	0	1	2	3	4
12. It is important for me to keep well away from weird or mentally unstable people.	0	1	2	3	4

Do you *disagree* or *agree* with the following statements?	Strongly disagree	Disagree	Neutral	Agree	Strongly agree
13. It scares me when my skin feels all prickly.	0	1	2	3	4
14. If I feel very contaminated, I get nervous that I might become mentally unstable.	0	1	2	3	4
15. For me it is much safer to eat fruit that has a removable skin.	0	1	2	3	4
16. I pick up illnesses far more easily than do other people.	0	1	2	3	4
17. Other people can tell if I feel contaminated.	0	1	2	3	4
18. If a weird or mentally unstable person comes close to me, I get very nervous.	0	1	2	3	4
19. If food is not completely fresh, I can tell right away.	0	1	2	3	4
20. I am extremely sensitive to tastes.	0	1	2	3	4
21. It scares me if I feel contaminated.	0	1	2	3	4
22. I worry about picking up some illness whenever I visit a hospital.	0	1	2	3	4
23. Unusual sensations on my skin make me very nervous.	0	1	2	3	4
24. I am extremely sensitive to smells.	0	1	2	3	4

Appendix 5

Personal Significance Scale (Intrusive Thoughts)

Please read the following statements carefully and circle the number that best corresponds to the extent to which you agree with each statement regarding your intrusive thoughts and images.

Specific thoughts and images: _____

_____

_____

_____

_____

Please use the following scale:

0	1	2	3	4	5	6	7	8
Not at all			Somewhat				Totally/definitely	

1.	Are these thoughts really personally significant for you?	0 1 2 3 4 5 6 7 8
2.	Do these thoughts reveal something important about you?	0 1 2 3 4 5 6 7 8
3.	Are these thoughts a sign that you are original?	0 1 2 3 4 5 6 7 8
4.	Do these thoughts mean that you might lose control and do something awful?	0 1 2 3 4 5 6 7 8
5.	Do these thoughts mean that you are an imaginative person?	0 1 2 3 4 5 6 7 8
6.	Do these thoughts mean that you might go crazy one day?	0 1 2 3 4 5 6 7 8
7.	Is it important for you to keep these thoughts secret from most or all of the people you know?	0 1 2 3 4 5 6 7 8
8.	Do these thoughts mean that you are a sensitive person?	0 1 2 3 4 5 6 7 8
9.	Do these thoughts mean that you are a dangerous person?	0 1 2 3 4 5 6 7 8
10.	Do these thoughts mean that you are untrustworthy?	0 1 2 3 4 5 6 7 8
11.	Would other people condemn or criticize you if they knew about your thoughts?	0 1 2 3 4 5 6 7 8

	0	1	2	3	4	5	6	7	8
Not at all					**Somewhat**				**Totally/definitely**

12.	Do these thoughts mean that you are really a hypocrite?	0 1 2 3 4 5 6 7 8
13.	Do these thoughts mean that you have an artistic talent?	0 1 2 3 4 5 6 7 8
14.	Would other people think that you are crazy or mentally unstable if they knew about your thoughts?	0 1 2 3 4 5 6 7 8
15.	Do these thoughts mean that one day you may actually carry out some actions related to the thoughts?	0 1 2 3 4 5 6 7 8
16.	Do these thoughts mean that you enjoy the company of other people?	0 1 2 3 4 5 6 7 8
17.	Do these thoughts mean that you are a bad, wicked person?	0 1 2 3 4 5 6 7 8
18.	Do you feel responsible for these thoughts?	0 1 2 3 4 5 6 7 8
19.	Is it important for you to cancel out or block the thoughts?	0 1 2 3 4 5 6 7 8
20.	Would other people think that you are a bad, wicked person if they knew about your thoughts?	0 1 2 3 4 5 6 7 8
21.	Do you think that you should avoid certain people or places because of these thoughts?	0 1 2 3 4 5 6 7 8
22.	Do these thoughts mean that you are weird?	0 1 2 3 4 5 6 7 8
23.	Should you fight against and resist these thoughts?	0 1 2 3 4 5 6 7 8
24.	Do these thoughts have any other significance for you? Details:	

_____

_____

25. What caused your thoughts to occur when they started?

_____

_____

26. Why do these thoughts keep coming back?

_____

_____

This Scale is designed to assess important interpretations of the intrusive thoughts, and how they change during treatment. It is a self-correcting scale, and if little or no positive changes are taking place during therapy, the need for a re-analysis of the problem and the treatment plan is recommended. Once the main misinterpretations have been identified, each is analysed in depth. This includes the patient's spontaneous interpretations, strength of belief, evidence and reasons for the interpretation, contrary evidence and reasons, spontaneous methods of resisting the thoughts and their efficacy, and effects of formal treatment.

After completing this detailed appraisal of the significance, proceed to an analysis of the evidence for and against the significance, and the reasons for and against the significance. As an aid, this Scale can promote an initial evaluation of the foundations and scaffolding that support the catastrophic interpretations.

This is primarily a qualitative scale, but, in some circumstances, mainly research, it is useful to score it. In order to discourage response sets, four buffer items are included, such as "Do these thoughts mean that you enjoy company?" These items should be deleted from any quantitative analysis—items 5, 8, 12, and 16.

Appendix 6

Contamination Standardized Interview Schedule

(Please use the schedule flexibly. Always try for details wherever possible.)

1 Are there any objects or places or substances that upset or scare you if you touch them—such as public washrooms, garbage bins, public telephones, insecticides, money, doorhandles, used bandages, blood or blood stains, greasy objects? Any others?

2 Do you attempt to avoid touching these items and places?

3 Please describe what happens if you do touch them.

4 Are there times when you can't seem to wash clean, no matter how hard you try?

5 Do you ever feel dirty or contaminated even though you haven't touched anything dirty or germy?

6 Do some things look clean but *feel* dirty?

7 Do *you* ever look clean but feel dirty?

8 Do you ever feel dirty *under* your skin?

9 When you feel contaminated, does it ever feel as if you are contaminated outside and *inside* your body?

10 Do you spend a lot of time washing and/or cleaning each day?

11 Do you ever feel contaminated without knowing why? Do you ever feel contaminated even though you *know* that you have not touched anything dirty or dangerous?

12 Can other people sense when you feel contaminated?

13 Are there any items or places in your own home or in the outside world that have been contaminated for a very long time (more than a year at least)?

14 In your home and outside, does the contamination spread from one object or person or place to another?

15 Do you try to keep your outdoor and indoor clothing strictly separate?

16 Are your feelings of contamination ever set off even without touching a contaminated object?

17 Are the feelings of contamination ever set off by memories?

18 Do you ever get feelings of dirtiness or contamination that are set off by having an unwanted, nasty, or repugnant thought?

19 Are the feelings of contamination ever set off by an upsetting remark or criticism of you?

20 Are the feelings of contamination associated with any particular person?

21 Are there any people whom you try to avoid touching, or being touched by, because of concerns about contamination?

22 If a weird or shabby or mentally unstable person comes close to you does it make you feel dirty or contaminated?

23 Does standing close to a person whom you feel can contaminate you ever make you feel dirty, even if there is no physical contact?

24 Do you ever worry that if you stare at or come too close to people who seem weird or mentally unstable you might begin to resemble them?

25 If you touch the clothing of someone whom you strongly dislike does it make you feel dirty or contaminated?

26 If you feel very contaminated do you get nervous that you might become crazy?

27 When you feel contaminated do you ever try to overcome the feelings by doing things in your head, such as counting, or praying, or trying to push away thoughts associated with the contamination? If yes, is it ever helpful?

28 Are your feelings of contamination ever accompanied by feelings of shame or guilt or anger?

29 Have you ever been contaminated by objects, places, or substances that did *not* contaminate other people?

30 Do you feel that you pick up contagious illnesses more easily than do other people?

31 When you are feeling contaminated do you try your very best to ensure that you don't pass the contamination on to other people?

32 For you, is the thought of passing contamination on to someone else much more frightening than yourself being contaminated?

33 If you have a thought about getting contaminated does it increase the risk that you will actually become contaminated?

34 Do you ever wake up in the morning feeling contaminated?

35 Some people feel that mental instability can be contagious and avoid contact with people who appear to be weird or mentally unstable. What do you think about that?

36 If you do something that you feel was bad or sinful, do you ever feel a strong urge to wash yourself thoroughly, all over?

37 If so, does the washing and/or showering make you feel a bit better about yourself?

38 Do some things look safe but *feel* dangerous?

Finally, therapist and patient combined—*What is the current threat?*

Treatment for OCD: Information for Patients

The psychological treatment for OCD is cognitive behavior therapy (CBT). Generally it takes about 12 one-hour sessions of individual therapy, with an interval of a week or so between sessions. In this therapy the nature and development of the OCD is traced and analysed and particular attention is given to the reasons why the patient currently feels under serious threat. The next step is to provide corrective information and carry out various therapeutic exercises.

Non-technical books, including self-help books, that provide comprehensive descriptions of the psychological treatment of all the various manifestations of this complex disorder are listed by Shafran et al. (2013), and the present description deals with fears of contamination and the consequent compulsive behavior, especially repetitive intensive washing and cleaning. Feelings of contamination can be extremely intense, demanding, and distressing and generate overwhelming urges to get rid of the contamination.

There are two forms of contamination fears. The familiar form, in which the feelings of contamination arise after touching a dirty/disgusting/dangerous object or item that is tangible (such as a discarded dirty bandage), is called *contact contamination*. The other form, *mental contamination*, develops when a person is psychologically and/or physically violated by another person. The feelings can be caused by a sexual assault or intensely humiliating or degrading experiences, such as a betrayal, and are easily evoked by disturbing memories, images, remarks, or insults—or anything or anyone associated with the violator. Unlike contact contamination this form of contamination can arise and be re-evoked without any physical contact with dirty or disgusting tangible objects. The source of mental contamination, however, is always a person, not an inanimate object.

The prevailing treatment of contact contamination involves repeated and prolonged exposures to the full range of contaminating stimuli. During and after the exposures, patients are firmly encouraged to refrain from carrying out any cleaning or washing. This exposure treatment (ERP—exposure and response prevention) is demanding but at least moderately effective.

Usually the therapist will have an account of the patient's problem from the referring source, supplemented by the results of psychological tests. If the presence of mental contamination is probable, a course of CBT is recommended. The initial sessions are devoted to tracing the development of the disorder, and, given that the patient will have experienced a significant physical or psychological violation, describing and talking about the people involved and the events that occurred, they tend to be highly emotional. Hence, a gentle gradual therapeutic approach is used.

As the therapy proceeds, specific techniques are introduced. These include the modification of distressing, recurrent, and unwanted images (pictures in the mind), testing out new ways of overcoming the unadaptive avoidance that accompanies this disorder, helping the patient to appraise the people who have had a major effect on their lives—such as the violator/s and also people who have been particularly kind, supportive, and helpful.

As the therapy sessions tend to be highly concentrated and busy, patients who wish to re-listen to the sessions are offered tapes or other recordings.

Appendix 8

Morphing: Information for Patients

Most feelings of contamination arise from direct contact with dirt/ disease or dangerous substances, and the unpleasant feelings can be removed by washing. Anxiety about becoming contaminated by people who are perceived to be weird/mentally unstable/immoral/disreputable is different.

The troubling feelings you experience when you get close to a weird person are *different* in important ways from feelings of familiar contamination that are caused by touching a dirty/dangerous substance. The undesirable, even dreaded characteristics of these people *cannot be transferred from one person to another*. You cannot pick up strange or weird behavior from touching, seeing, or coming close to a disturbed or undesirable person. It never happens.

The very idea of mental instability, drug addiction, or mental deterioration can be upsetting, and encountering a disturbed/weird person can evoke feelings of anxiety. Merely seeing a disturbed person can be upsetting, even without any contact, even when seen at some distance.

Do you think that your family can pick up mental instability in this way? Do you worry that your family or friends might be transformed by seeing or walking near an unstable/weird person? Most people who are affected by this psychological problem believe that they are *uniquely* at risk of picking up undesirable characteristics, addiction, or mental disturbance by mere proximity. There is no medical evidence that this can happen.

Healthcare workers who care for mentally disturbed people on a daily basis, the nurses, psychologists, and doctors, do not pick up mental instability from their patients. No transfer occurs. The same is true of undesirable characteristics. We do not pick them up by physical contact with people who manifest such characteristics. Personality characteristics, desirable and undesirable, evolve gradually from childhood into adulthood. They are not transferable by an incidental contact with a person one happens to come across.

The fear of being adversely affected by indirect or direct contact with weird-looking people, addicts, or mentally unstable people is called the "fear of morphing." It is treated by psychological therapy.

The majority of people who develop a fear of being adversely changed by contact with undesirable characteristics or people function tolerably well despite the problem and live ordinary lives. The thought that one might be changed adversely through direct or indirect contact with a weird-looking person can arise in many social situations (e.g., shops, buses), but the feared changes never take place. The problem is a problem of your *thoughts*, not a problem caused by a feared transformation into another person.

People who are affected by a fear of morphing recognize the irrational nature of their beliefs, and their friends and relatives are dismissive of the notion. However, they remain puzzled by the inconsistency between their beliefs and their strong reactions when they encounter strange/weird people. Not uncommonly they try to explain it by resorting to the notion that there are "mental germs" that are capable of transmitting undesirable changes in one's personality, or mental illnesses or psychological disturbances. They are re-assured that this worrying idea occurs in cases of morphing but that there is no scientific evidence to support it.

Some people get so concerned about picking up undesirable or harmful characteristics by proximity to a person who appears to be mentally unstable that they begin to fear they will contract a contagious mental illness and be ruined. But there is no medical evidence that mental illness is contagious, in the way that flu, measles, and chicken pox can be transferred by contact. Nurses and doctors who care for patients with a mental illness do not pick up the illnesses.

If there was a possibility of picking up undesirable personality characteristics from proximity to a disturbed person, repeatedly washing your hands would not solve the problem. Washing one's hands, however vigorously, has no effect on your personality. The idea of being affected by coming too close to a weird/strange person can be upsetting, but it is an idea, and upsetting ideas are not easily washed away.

This kind of fear is an unusual manifestation of OCD, which is a well-recognized psychological problem. Despite dozens or hundreds of encounters with "undesirable" people, you have not been harmed. You have not picked up any of their characteristics or weaknesses. You have had the fearful thoughts many, many times, but they have never been followed by the harm that you fear. Nothing has happened to you, you have not been changed. You are neither weird nor mentally unstable. *The problem you are dealing with is one of thoughts*, not events, or actions, or undesirable changes, or misfortunes.

These thoughts and fears are a sort of contamination, but not ordinary contamination, not the kind that occurs when we touch a dirty or diseased substance. It is called mental contamination and can be caused even without any physical contact with a dirty substance. It certainly is a feeling of dirtiness, but of a different kind. Even the mere sight of particular people can cause feelings of mental contamination; so can television shows, pictures, memories, and images. Mental contamination produces the same reactions as ordinary contamination—the need to wash and/or neutralize, and to avoid the source of the contamination. Your fear of picking up some undesirable or harmful characteristics from coming close to shabby/weird/unstable people is a form of mental contamination.

People who develop this fear generally have past or current fears of contamination, especially contact contamination that is provoked by touching dangerous or dirty substances. This is a common manifestation of OCD. Mostly they manage to live a moderately satisfying occupational, personal, and social life despite the intense uneasiness and fear of being tainted which they experience in the presence of particular people. It is distressing and frustrating but not disabling. When an encounter occurs it produces unpleasant feelings of contamination and an urge to wash away the contaminant, or to neutralize the feelings by going in for mental cleansing by counting or similar tactics. At best, the washing and neutralizing bring temporary relief, but leave the fear intact.

However, the fact that washing/neutralizing brings some relief confirms the presence of fear/anxiety. The washing does not ensure safety from the threat of changing, of morphing, but can ease the anxiety. It is best to inhibit the urges to avoid the "undesirable" people, and it is best to inhibit the urges to wash and neutralize.

It is helpful to compile a list of *your desirable and approved characteristics and beliefs* which are so well grounded and stable that they are most unlikely to ever change.

Self-Contamination: Information for Patients

In addition to the familiar form of contamination that occurs after touching a dirty/disgusting/diseased object, people can develop feelings of contamination even without physically touching a contaminant. Sometimes it happens after having certain thoughts or images, and can cause such intense feelings of contamination that the person has to wash them away. Many patients are surprised to learn that feelings of contamination can even be aroused by thoughts, their own thoughts. Like most of us, they know that contamination occurs after touching a nasty tangible substance. However, the evocation of feelings of contamination can also occur without touching anything. (The information can be reinforced by simple demonstrations in which the patient is asked to observe the effects of forming vivid images of the contaminating people or cues, and by the deliberate recall of significant episodes of contamination.)

Virtually everyone experiences unwanted intrusive thoughts and, for the most part, they are simply dismissed. However, if the intrusions are interpreted as being highly significant and even revealing of the person's fundamental personality, difficulties can arise. The mis-appraisals of the significance of the intrusions tend to be so upsetting that the person feels compelled to block or suppress the unwelcome, tormenting thoughts. Unfortunately this rarely helps and often increases the frequency of the obsessions, leaving the person feeling polluted and wretched.

Certain obsessions are prone to induce feelings of self-contamination. Repugnant sexual obsessions, such as molesting a child and incestuous images, are prime examples. If the images, or dreams, are misinterpreted as expressions of objectionable intentions, the person may think that the obsessions reveal a lurking, repulsive part of their true character, and feel polluted. The feelings of internal dirtiness and pollution instigate attempts at physical and/or mental cleansing.

Obsessions in which the person fears that he/she might attack or harm someone, known or unknown, can also generate feelings of self-contamination. These intrusive feelings can be exceedingly distressing. As the source of the contamination, one's self, is always present, the threat of re-contamination is constant. There is no period of safety. See Table A.1.

Table A.1 Behavior Experiment Record Sheet

Situation	Predictions	Experiment	Outcome	What I learned
	What do I think will actually happen?	What can I do to test my fear of contamination?	What actually happened?	What do I make of the experiment?
	How much do I believe it will (0–100%)?	How can I find out what will happen to my fear?	Were any of my predictions correct?	How much do I believe my initial predictions will happen in the future (0–100%)?
	What will happen to my fear of contamination?			How can I test this further?
	How much do I believe this (0–100%)?			

References

Abramowitz, J., Whiteside, S., Lynman, D., and Kalsy, S. (2003). Is thought-action fusion specific to obsessive-compulsive disorder? A mediating role of negative affect. *Behaviour Research and Therapy, 41*, 1069–1079.

Adams, T., Badour,C., Cister, J., and Feldner, M. (2014). Contamination aversion and post-traumatic severity following sexual trauma. *Cognitive Therapy and Research.* Doi 10.1007/s 10608-014-9609-9.

Anand, M. (1940). *Untouchable.* London, Penguin Books.

Antony, M., Downie, F., and Swinson, R. (1998). Diagnostic issues and epidemiology in Obsessive Compulsive Disorder. In: *Obsessive Compulsive Disorder: Theory, Research and Treatment*, edited by R. Swinson, M. Antony, S. Rachman, and M. Richter. Chapter 1. New York, Guilford Press.

Arntz, A., Rauner, M., and van den Hout, M. (1995). "If I feel anxious, there must be danger": ex-consequential reasoning in inferring danger in anxiety disorders. *Behaviour Research and Therapy, 33*, 917–925.

Arntz, A., Tiesema, M., and Kindt, M. (2007). Treatment of PTSD: a comparison of imaginal exposure with and without imagery rescripting. *Journal of Behaviour Therapy and Experimental Psychiatry, 38*, 345–370.

Ayto, J. (1990). *Dictionary of Word Origins.* New York, Arcade Publishing.

Badour, C., Feldner, M., Babson, K., Blumenthal, H., and Dutton, C. (2012). Disgust, mental contamination, and post-traumatic stress; unique relations following sexual versus non-sexual assault. *Journal of Anxiety Disorders, 27*, 155–162.

Beck, A.T. (1976). *Cognitive Therapy and the Emotional Disorders.* New York, International Universities Press.

Beck, A.T., Steer, R.A., and Brown, G.K. (1996). *Manual for the Beck Depression Inventory-II.* San Antonio, Texas, Psychological Corporation.

Berle, D. and Starcevic, V. (2005). Thought-action fusion: review of the literature and future directions. *Clinical Psychology Review, 25*, 263–284.

Berman, N., Wheaton, M., and Abramowitz, J. (2012). The "Arnold Schwarzenegger Effect": is strength of the "victim" related to misinterpretations of harm intrusions? *Behaviour Research and Therapy, 50*, 761–766.

Boschen, M. (2013). Differences in effectiveness of physical and mental washing in reducing mental contamination. In: New research developments in the psychological understanding of OCD, M. Toffolo (Chair). Symposium at the 2013 EABCT conference, Marrakech, Morocco.

Breuer, J. and Freud, S. (1895, 1957 edition). *Studies on Hysteria.* New York, Basic Books.

Bunyan, J. (1998, Oxford Edition). *Grace Abounding to the Chief of Sinners (1666)*. Oxford, Oxford University Press.

Clark, D.A. (2004). *Cognitive-Behavior Therapy for OCD*. New York, Guilford.

Clark, D.A. and Beck, A.T. (2011). *Cognitive Therapy of Anxiety Disorders: Science and Practice*. New York, Guilford Press.

Clark, D.A. and Purdon, C. (1993). New perspectives for a cognitive theory of obsessions. *Australian Psychologist*, *28*, 161–167.

Clark, D.M. (1986). A cognitive approach to panic. *Behaviour Research and Therapy*, *24*, 461–470.

Clark, D.M. and Fairburn, C. (eds) (1997). *Science and Practice of Cognitive Behaviour Therapy*. Oxford, Oxford University Press.

Clark, D.M. and Wells, A. (1995). A cognitive model of social phobia. In *Social Phobia: Diagnosis, Assessment, Treatment*, edited by R.G. Heimberg et al., Chapter 4. New York, Guilford Press.

Coughtrey, A.E., Shafran, R., Knibbs, D., and Rachman, S.J. (2012a). Mental contamination in obsessive-compulsive disorder. *Journal of Obsessive Compulsive and Related Disorders*, *1*, 244–250.

Coughtrey, A.E., Shafran, R., Lee, M., and Rachman, S.J. (2012b). It's the feeling inside my head: a qualitative analysis of mental contamination in obsessive-compulsive disorder. *Behavioural and Cognitive Psychotherapy*, *40*, 163–173.

Coughtrey, A.E., Shafran, R., Lee, M., and Rachman, S.J. (2013a). The treatment of mental contamination: a case series. *Cognitive and Behavioural Practice*, *20*, 221–231.

Coughtrey, A.E., Shafran, R., and Rachman, S.J. (2013b). Imagery in mental contamination: a questionnaire study. *Journal of Obsessive-Compulsive and Related Disorders*, *2*, 385–390.

Coughtrey, A.E., Shafran, R., and Rachman, S.J. (2014a). The spread of mental contamination. *Journal of Behaviour Therapy and Experimental Psychiatry*, *45*, 33–38.

Coughtrey, A.E., Shafran, R., and Rachman, S.J. (2014b). The spontaneous decay and persistence of mental contamination: an experimental analysis. *Journal of Behaviour Therapy and Experimental Psychiatry*, *45*, 90–96.

Craske, M. (2003). *Origin of Phobias and Anxiety Disorders: Why More Women Than Men?* Oxford, Elsevier Press.

Deacon, B. and Olatunji, B. (2007). Specificity of disgust sensitivity in the prediction of behavioural avoidance in contamination fears. *Behaviour Research and Therapy*, *45*, 2110–2120.

de Silva, P. and Marks, M. (1999). The role of traumatic experiences in the genesis of OCD. *Behaviour Research and Therapy*, *37*, 941–951.

Douglas, M. (1966). *Purity and Danger*. London, Routledge and Kegan Paul.

Eddy, K., Dutra, L., Bradley, R., and Westen, D. (2004). A multi-dimensional meta-analysis of psychotherapy and pharmacotherapy for OCD. *Clinical Psychology Review*, *24*, 1011–1030.

Edwards, S. and Salkovskis, P. (2005). An experimental demonstration that fear, but not disgust, is associated with a return of fear in phobias. *Journal of Anxiety Disorders*, *20*, 58–71.

Ehlers, A. and Clark, D.M. (2000). A cognitive model of PTSD. *Behaviour Research and Therapy*, *115*, 319–345.

Ehlers, A., Clark, D., Hackmann, A., McManus, F., and Fenell, M. (2005). Cognitive therapy for PTSD: development and evaluation. *Behaviour Research and Therapy*, *43*, 413–432.

Ehlers, A., Clark, D.M., Hankmann, A., McManus, F., Fennell, M., Herbert, C., et al. (2003). A randomised controlled trial of cognitive therapy, a self-help booklet, and repeated assessments as early interventions for posttraumatic stress disorder. *Archives of General Psychiatry*, *60*, 1024–1032.

Ehlers, A., Grey, N., Wild, J., Stott, R., Liness, S., Deale, A., et al. (2013). Implementation of cognitive therapy for PTSD in routine clinical care: effectiveness and moderators of outcome in a consecutive sample. *Behaviour Research and Therapy*, *51*, 742–752.

Elliott, C.M. and Radomsky, A.S. (2009). Analyses of mental contamination: Part I, experimental manipulations of morality. *Behaviour Research and Therapy*, *47*, 995–1003.

Elliott, C.M. and Radomsky, A.S. (2013). Meaning and mental contamination: focus on appraisals. *Clinical Psychologist*, *17*(1), 17–25.

Fairbrother, N., Newth, S., and Rachman, S. (2005). Mental pollution: feelings of dirtiness without physical contact. *Behaviour Research and Therapy*, *43*, 121–130.

Fairbrother, N. and Rachman, S. (2004). Feelings of mental pollution subsequent to sexual assault. *Behaviour Research and Therapy*, *42*, 173–190.

Foa, E.B., Huppert, J.D., Leiberg, S., Langner, R., Kichic, R., Hajcak, G., et al. (2002). The obsessive-compulsive inventory: development and validation of a short version. *Psychological Assessment*, *14*, 485–496.

Foa, E., Liebowitz, M., Kozak, M., Davies, S., Campeas, R., Franklin, M.E., et al. (2005). Randomized, placebo-controlled trial of exposure and ritual prevention, clomipramine and their combination in the treatment of OCD. *American Journal of Psychiatry*, *162*, 151–161.

Frazer, J.G. (1922). *The Golden Bough. New York, Criterion Press* (1999 edition, Touchstone Press, New York).

Freeston, M., Ladouceur, R., Gagnon, F., Thibodiau, N., Rheaume, J., Letarte, H., et al. (1997). Cognitive behavioral treatment of obsessive thoughts: a controlled study. *Journal of Consulting and Clinical Psychology*, *65*, 405–413.

Freud, S. (1895, 1957 edition). Frau Emmy von N. (Freud), pp. 48–105. In: *Studies on Hysteria*, edited by J. Breuer and S. Freud. New York, Basic Books.

Gershuny, B., Baer, L., Radomsky, A.,Wilson, K., and Jenike, M. (2003). Connections among symptoms of OCD and PTSD: a case series. *Behaviour Research and Therapy*, *41*, 1029–1042.

Hackmann, A., Bennet-Levy, J., and Holmes, E. (2011). *Imagery in Cognitive Therapy.* Oxford, Oxford University Press.

Herba, J. (2005). Individual differences in psychological feelings of contamination. M.A. Dissertation, University of British Columbia.

Herba, J. and Rachman, S. (2007). Vulnerability to mental contamination. *Behaviour Research and Therapy, 45,* 2804–2812.

Hodgson, R. and Rachman, S. (1977). Obsessional compulsive complaints. *Behaviour Research and Therapy, 15,* 389–395.

Homer (2003 edition). *The Odyssey.* Translated by E.V. Rieu. London, Penguin Classics.

Human Rights Watch Report (1999). *Broken People: Caste Violence Against India's "Untouchables."* New York, Human Rights Watch Publication.

Ishikawa, R., Kobori, O., and Shimizu, E. (2013). Unwanted sexual experiences and cognitive appraisals that evoke mental contamination. *Behavioural and Cognitive Psychotherapy, 7,* 1–15.

Jacobi, D., Daflos, S., and Whittal, M. (2014). Cognitive and behaviour therapy in group and individual treatment of OCD: a subtype evaluation. In preparation.

Kafka, F. (1983 Penguin edition). The metamorphosis (1912). In: *The Penguin Complete Stories of Franz Kafka.* London, Penguin Books.

Kahneman, D. (2011). *Thinking, Fast and Slow.* Toronto, Doubleday.

Kuyken, W., Padesky, C.A., and Dudley, R. (2009). *Collaborative Case Conceptualisation.* New York, Guilford Press.

Lambert, M.J., Whipple, J.L., Smart, D.W., Vermeersch, D.A., and Nielsen, S.L. (2001). The effects of providing therapists with feedback on patient progress during psychotherapy: are outcomes enhanced? *Psychotherapy Research, 11,* 49–68.

Lang, P. (1985). The cognitive psychophysiology of emotion. In: *Anxiety and the Anxiety Disorders,* edited by A. Tuma and J. Maser. Hillsdale, Erlbaum Associates.

Lipton, M., Brewin, C., Luke, S., and Halperin, J. (2010). Distinguishing features of intrusive images in OCD. *Journal of Anxiety Disorders, 24,* 816–822.

Melli, G., Bulli, F., Carraresi, C., and Stopani, E. (2014). Disgust propensity and contamination-related symptoms: the mediating role of mental contamination. *Journal of Obsessive-Compulsive and Related Disorders, 3,* 77–82.

Obsessive Compulsive Cognitions Working Group (2003). Psychometric validation of the Obsessive Beliefs Questionnaire and the Interpretation of Intrusions Inventory: Part 1. *Behaviour Research and Therapy, 41,* 863–878.

O'Sullivan, G. and Marks, I. (1991). Follow-up studies of behavioral treatment of phobic and obsessive-compulsive neuroses. *Psychiatric Annals, 21,* 368–373.

Poulton, R. and Menzies, R. (2002). Non-associative fear acquisition: a review of the retrospective and longitudinal research. *Behaviour Research and Therapy, 40,* 127–150.

Rachman, S. (1978). *Fear and Courage.* San Francisco, W.H. Freeman.

Rachman, S. (1990). *Fear and Courage*, 2nd edn. New York, W.H. Freeman.

Rachman, S. (1994). Pollution of the mind. *Behaviour Research and Therapy, 32*, 311–314.

Rachman, S. (1997a). A cognitive theory of obsessions. *Behaviour Research and Therapy, 35*, 793–802.

Rachman, S. (1997b). The evolution of cognitive behaviour therapy. In: *The Science and Practice of Cognitive Behaviour Therapy*, edited by D.M. Clark and C. Fairburn. Oxford, Oxford University Press.

Rachman, S. (1998). A cognitive theory of obsessions: elaborations. *Behaviour Research and Therapy, 36*, 385–401.

Rachman, S. (2002). A cognitive theory of compulsive checking. *Behaviour Research and Therapy, 40*, 625–639.

Rachman, S. (2003). *The Treatment of Obsessions*. Oxford, Oxford University Press.

Rachman, S. (2006). *Fear of Contamination*. Oxford, Oxford University Press.

Rachman, S. (2007). Unwanted intrusive images in obsessive-compulsive disorders. *Journal of Behaviour Therapy and Experimental Psychiatry, 38*, 402–410.

Rachman, S. (2010). Betrayal: a psychological analysis. *Behaviour Research and Therapy, 48*, 304–311

Rachman, S. (2013a). Cleaning damned spots from the obsessive mind. *Nature, 503*, 7, November.

Rachman, S. (2013b). *Anxiety*, 3rd edn. Hove, Psychology Press.

Rachman, S., Cobb, C., Grey, S., McDonald, B., and Sartory, G. (1979). Behavioural treatment of obsessional compulsive disorder, with and without clomipramine. *Behaviour Research and Therapy, 17*, 467–478.

Rachman, S. and de Silva, P. (1978). Abnormal and normal obsessions. *Behaviour Research and Therapy, 16*, 233–248.

Rachman, S. and Hodgson, R. (1980). *Obsessions and Compulsions*. Englewood, New Jersey, Prentice Hall.

Rachman, S., Radomsky, A.S., Elliot, C.M., and Zysk, E. (2012). Mental contamination: the perpetrator effect. *Journal of Behaviour Therapy and Experimental Psychiatry, 43*, 587–593.

Rachman, S., Radomsky, A., and Hammond, D. (2003). The judicious use of safety gear in overcoming a fear of snakes. Unpublished manuscript, University of British Columbia.

Rachman, S., Radomsky, A., Shafran, R., and Zysk, E. (2011). Reducing contamination by exposure plus safety behaviour. *Journal of Behaviour Therapy and Experimental Psychiatry, 42*, 397–404.

Rachman, S. and Shafran, R. (1998). Cognitive and behavioural features of obsessive-compulsive disorder. In: *Obsessive-Compulsive Disorder: Theory, Research, and Treatment*, edited by R. Swinson, M. Antony, S. Rachman, and M. Richter, Chapter 3. New York, Guilford Press.

Radomsky, A.S. and Elliott, C.M. (2009). Analyses of mental contamination: Part II, individual differences. *Behaviour Research and Therapy, 47*, 1004–1011.

Radomsky, A.S., Gilchrist, P.T., and Dussault, D. (2006a). Repeated checking really does cause memory distrust. *Behaviour Research and Therapy, 44*, 305–316.

Radomsky, A.S., Ouimet, A.J., Ashbaugh, A.R., Lavoie, S.L., Parrish, C.L., and O'Connor, K.P. (2006b). Psychometric properties of the French and English versions of the Vancouver Obsessional Compulsive Inventory and the Symmetry, Ordering and Arranging Questionnaire. *Cognitive Behaviour Therapy, 35*, 164–173.

Radomsky, A. and Rachman, S. (1999). Memory bias in OCD. *Behaviour Research and Therapy, 37*, 605–618.

Radomsky, A.S., Rachman, S., Shafran, R., Coughtrey, A.E., and Barber, K.C. (2014). The nature and assessment of mental contamination: a psychometric analysis. *Journal of Obsessive Compulsive and Related Disorders, 3*(2), 181–187.

Rasmussen, S. and Eisen, J. (1992). The epidemiology and clinical features of OCD. *Psychiatric Clinics of North America, 15*, 743–758.

Rassin, E. (2006). *Thought Suppression*. Oxford, Elsevier Press.

Rees, C., Austen, T., and Anderson, R. (2013). Can corrective information reduce negative appraisals of intrusive thoughts? *Behavioural and Cognitive Psychotherapy, 42*, 502–507.

Ricciardi, J. and McNally, R. (1995). Depressed mood is related to obsessions, but not to compulsions in OCD. *Journal of Anxiety Disorders, 9*, 249–256.

Rozin, P. and Fallon, A. (1987). A perspective on disgust. *Psychological Review, 94*, 23–41.

Salkovskis, P. (1985). Obsessional compulsive problems: a cognitive behavioural analysis. *Behaviour Research and Therapy, 23*, 571–583.

Sawchuk, C., Lohr, J., Tolin, D., Lee, T., and Kleinknecht, R. (2000). Disgust sensitivity and contamination fears in spider and blood-injection-injury phobias. *Behaviour Research and Therapy, 38*, 753–762.

Shafran, R., Brosan, L., and Cooper, P. (2013). *The Complete CBT Guide for Anxiety*. London, Constable and Robinson.

Shafran, R. and Rachman, S. (2004). Thought-action-fusion: a review. *Journal of Behavior Therapy and Experimental Psychiatry, 35*, 87–108.

Shafran, R. and Radomsky, A.S. (2013). Obsessive compulsive disorder. In: *The Complete CBT Guide for Anxiety*, edited by R. Shafran, L. Brosan, and P. Cooper, Chapter 11. London, Constable and Robinson.

Shafran, R., Thordarson, D.S., and Rachman, S.J. (1996). Thought-action fusion in obsessive-compulsive disorder. *Journal of Anxiety Disorders, 10*, 379–391.

Steil, R., Jung, K., and Stangier, U. (2011). Efficacy of a two-session program of cognitive restructuring and imagery modification to reduce the feeling of being contaminated in adult survivors of childhood sexual abuse: a pilot study. *Journal of Behaviour Therapy and Experimental Psychiatry, 42*, 325–329.

Sutherland, G., Newman, B., and Rachman, S. (1983). Experimental investigations of the relations between mood and unwanted intrusive cognitions. *British Journal of Medical Psychology*, 55, 127–135.

Tallis, F. (1997). The neuropsychology of OCD. *British Journal of Clinical Psychology*, 36, 3–20.

Taylor, S.E. (1989). *Positive Illusions*. New York, Basic Books.

Thordarson, D.S., Radomsky, A.S., Rachman, S.J., Shafran, R., Sawchuk, C.N., and Hakstian, A.R. (2004). The Vancouver Obsessional Compulsive Inventory (VOCI). *Behaviour Research and Therapy*, 42, 1289–1314.

Tolin, D., Worhunsky, P., and Maltby, N. (2004). Sympathetic magic in contamination-related OCD. *Journal of Behaviour Therapy and Experimental Psychiatry*, 35, 193–205.

van Balkom, A.J., Emmelkamp, P.M., Eikelenboom, M., Hoogendoom, A.W., Smit, J.H., and van Oppen, P. (2012). Cognitive therapy versus fluvoxamine as a second-step treatment in obsessive-compulsive disorder nonresponsive to first-step behaviour therapy. *Psychotherapy and Psychosomatics*, 81, 366–374.

Van den Hout, M. and Kindt, M. (2003). Repeated checking causes memory distrust. *Behaviour Research and Therapy*, 41, 301–316.

Vos, S., Huibers, M., and Arntz, A. (2012). Experimental investigation of targeting responsibility vs danger in cognitive therapy of OCD. *Depression and Anxiety*, 29, 629–637.

Ware, J., Jain, K., Burgess, I., and Davey, G. (1994). Disease-avoidance model: factor analysis of common animal fears. *Behaviour Research and Therapy*, 32, 57–63.

Whittal, M.L., Woody, S.R., McLean, P.D., Rachman, S.J., and Robichaud, M. (2010). Treatment of obsessions: a randomised controlled trial. *Behaviour Research and Therapy*, 48, 295–303.

Woody, S. and Teachman, B. (2000). Intersection of disgust and fear: normative and pathological views. *Clinical Psychology Science and Practice*, 7, 291–311.

Wroe, A.L. and Salkovskis, P.M. (2000). Causing harm and allowing harm: a study of beliefs in obsessional problems. *Behaviour Research and Therapy*, 38, 1141–1162.

Zucker, B.G. (2004). Early intervention for sub-clinical OCD. PhD Thesis, University of California at Los Angeles.

Index

Printed in Great Britain
by Amazon.co.uk, Ltd.,
Marston Gate.